THE
UNFLUSTERED
MOM

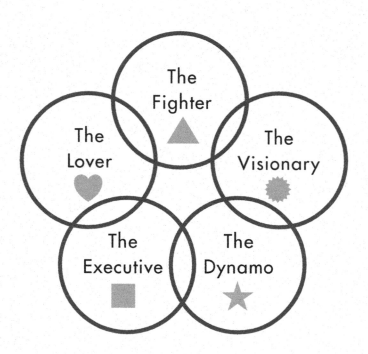

THE
UNFLUSTERED
MOM

HOW UNDERSTANDING

THE **FIVE ANXIETY STYLES**

TRANSFORMS THE **WAY WE**

PARENT, PARTNER, LIVE, AND **LOVE**

Amber Trueblood

CHICAGO

Published by Parenting Press
An imprint of Chicago Review Press Incorporated
814 North Franklin Street
Chicago, Illinois 60610
ISBN 978-1-64160-886-2

Library of Congress Control Number: 2023902685

Cover design: Natalya Balnova
Typesetting: Nord Compo

Printed in the United States of America

"World peace must develop from inner peace. Peace is not just mere absence of violence. Peace is, I think, the manifestation of human compassion."

—Dalai Lama XIV

CONTENTS

Part I: Unflustering

1 The Five Flourish Types 3
2 The Secret Life of Moms. 15
3 Socks and Shoes. 27

Part II: From Anxiety Styles to Flourish Types

4 The Lover ♥ 47
5 The Visionary ✺ 63
6 The Dynamo ★ 75
7 The Executive ■ 90
8 The Fighter ▲ 103

Part III: Flourishing

9 Knowing Yourself 117
10 Creating Your Plan 134
11 Talking with Words. 150
12 Your Fluster Is Totally Flustering My Fluster! 168

Farewell to Fluster 197

PART I

UNFLUSTERING

1

THE FIVE FLOURISH TYPES

I REMEMBER LYING AWAKE ONE NIGHT, imagining a house fire. I mentally orchestrated how I would get my four little ones out of the house safely. My husband was working nights at the time. I decided I'd put one on each hip, lay two on a blanket, then drag the blanket down the hall and out the front door. As a mother of four sons, I am only one of many moms who juggle the many worries and multiple responsibilities of mom life. We are the referees, social planners, medics, financial consultants, cooks, travel agents, educational specialists, family therapists, and housekeepers. Heck, I even started cutting my boys' hair because it's cheaper and easier than dragging everyone to a barber shop. It's all utterly exhausting.

Actually, it's not *just* exhausting. It's a nonstop state of being "on" 24/7, of tending to, managing, and supporting our children, our partners, our careers, and our households. Oh, and if there's time, we try to take care of our own physical and mental health—and maybe also clean out all the dirty socks stuck behind the washing machine. This nonstop pressure affects our jobs, our parenting, our finances, our relationships, and our emotional well-being. It certainly doesn't make sleep any easier either. I like to use the word *flustered* for the moms I coach. In the mild version of flustered, we feel tired, resentful, or frustrated. In the extreme version, we feel exhausted, anxious, or angry. The word *fluster* literally means "a state of agitated confusion." It's believed to be of Scandinavian origin because of its similarity to the Icelandic word *flaustr* meaning "hurry" or *flaustra* meaning "to bustle." When moms hurry and bustle constantly, everyone suffers. Children suffer. Relationships suffer. Friendships suffer. Careers suffer. Health suffers. And the ability to find joy and fulfillment in our lives suffers.

Most of us don't have access to the support or resources we need to manage our *flusterment* in a healthier way. Social media platforms like Instagram and Facebook add a nice helping of unrealistic expectations to our guilt and self-judgment. Women end up with symptoms ranging from "mom guilt" and "mommy brain" to depression, anxiety, panic attacks, substance abuse, and eating disorders. Moms are more flustered now than ever before.

When moms can't manage their frustrations in a healthy way, we argue more with our partners, drink more, eat more, or begin to isolate ourselves. How can we expect moms to raise the next generation of responsible citizens and compassionate leaders when we feel ridiculously overwhelmed and physically exhausted? The pages that follow will offer you insights and practical tools to better manage your daily flusters, dismantle your unhealthy beliefs, and celebrate your supermom powers. (Because I'm certain you're not giving yourself proper credit for all the places you're killing it!)

The insights and strategies in this book will allow you to take control of your life, fully and confidently. You're going to learn how to release your guilt, wipe away your worries, and smash the anxiety in your life.

> ## Get the tools you need to create
> ## the life you want and deserve.

While we'll always have a reason to feel flustered, we can learn how to prepare, manage, and respond to life's challenges in much healthier ways. That's what you'll learn here, if you're ready for it.

Anxiety

What is anxiety really? When you're anxious, you imagine the future is bad, that proverbial monsters are lurking just out of view around the next bend. When you're excited, you think the future might be great, that champagne and chocolate truffles are just around the corner! It's all about perception. What do you *feel* might happen? If it's good stuff, start the confetti and alert the excitement area of your brain! If it's bad stuff, call in the reinforcements and ready your weapons. Our emotional state depends on our interpretation. What do we think might happen next?

You've probably heard that many highly successful musicians and performers feel pre-show jitters. Are they anxious or are they *excited*? Anxiety and excitement look very similar on a physiological level. Seasoned performers typically interpret their feelings as excitement. They don't stand around waiting until they feel calm to go on stage. No, they've learned to think of those butterflies and sweaty palms as excitement rather than nerves. I love entrepreneur and philanthropist Marie Forleo's take on it. She says, "Fear is excitement with the brakes on. It's just energy. Fear can be instructive and directive. It's a guide that'll show you exactly where you have to go."

As humans, our attention is naturally drawn to the worst-case scenario. We are wired to *survive* more than we're wired to *thrive*. If our ancestors had been wired differently, we simply wouldn't be here to witness it. Unfortunately, there are two problems with this wiring: (1) our perceptions aren't always right, and (2) living in a near-constant state of anxiety is not good for our bodies, brains, or our emotional health. The good news: you are smarter and wiser than the Neanderthal parts of your brain, and because of that, you can outsmart your wiring so that you can both survive *and* thrive.

Fear and Stress

Here's how fear works in your body: When one of your senses (or even your imagination) receives potentially threatening information, several things happen very quickly. Your body releases hormones to signal the shutdown of any functions not necessary for your immediate survival, like your digestive tract and your immune system. Any functions that support immediate survival then become amplified. They go on high alert. Your eyesight and hearing become more acute. Your heart rate increases. Blood rushes to your extremities in case you need to run or fight. You become hyper-focused on the threat (or perceived threat), since getting distracted by a pretty butterfly or randomly pondering what to get your mom for her birthday next week just might get you killed.

Stress is the modern-day response to these primal fears of perceived threat. And long periods under stressful conditions, like motherhood for instance, can wreak havoc on us physically and psychologically. Meditation expert and mom Emily Fletcher says, "Stress is a bully. Stress keeps your body and your mind trapped in a place of perpetual unrest, worry, and discontent; it keeps you on edge, feeling nervous, and always looking over your shoulder—exactly like a playground tyrant."

Remaining in a stressful state for long periods can cause major damage to the body. In prehistoric days, it was unlikely crocodiles would attack every hour throughout your day. Right? One big scare every few days or weeks would probably be enough to get you to move to a different area of the savanna. Your physiology was not designed to endure 24 crocodile attacks a day. No, your body needs time to build up the hormonal reserves and provide sufficient oxygen and blood to your brain and internal organs so that you can survive the next potential attack in a few weeks.

Unfortunately, your brain responds to losing your keys or stepping on a tiny Lego almost the same as it would respond to a swarm of killer bees in your backyard. Even if you *think* you see killer bees, it's far more likely to be a cluster of those poofy white dandelion seeds flying around. It might feel scary at the moment, but your biggest *real* concern is they all land in your hair and now you can't tell the difference between your gray roots and the dandelion poofs. Life in recent times leaves us all constantly mistaking innocuous situations for real threats. (I mean seriously, dandelions are edible, so if anything they should be scared of us!) Our once-useful propensity to imagine the worst is now exhausting. We're in a near-perpetual state of fight or flight. Add in lack of sleep, and it's miraculous we're functioning at all.

Stress Is Good . . . *Sometimes*

When we talk about stress and anxiety, we often act like it's all bad. Frankly, our minds and our bodies *need* stress. For instance, exercise is simply a short-term stressor for our muscles and our cardiovascular system. It's enduring an extended period under stressful conditions that does the real damage. The stress we grow and learn from, called *eustress*, we need that. Stress that depletes and damages us, that's destructive stress.

The problem with bad stress is that even moderate or mild levels can do a lot of damage. Feeling constantly flustered and overwhelmed is a serious problem. Sure, you can handle it. No, it won't kill you. But listen closely, my friend. Months or years functioning in this highly flustered state can cause physiological, physical, and psychological problems. Many moms downplay the stress they're under. We see other people who are dealing with bigger problems, so we discount our "minor" stressors, right? We call them petty. And we use that to avoid asking for the help we need and deserve. Just because there are children who live in food deserts, with no access to fresh food, doesn't mean that we stop feeding our children fresh food if we have access to it. "That other mom has a much bigger swarm of bees chasing her. And, crap! It looks like they're actual bees and not seeds. So I'll just keep quiet and endure." Listen, when you discount your own struggles, you don't give yourself the chance to get the help you need. Your body and mind don't get a break. And how is that helping the other mom with the real bees? Maybe you try to muscle through it, distract yourself with a pint of Ben & Jerry's Vanilla Caramel Fudge. You'll relax when you die, right? *Wrong.*

Our bodies are not wired to endure long periods under stressful conditions. Whether stress involves a real, physical threat or a perceived threat doesn't matter at all. To your brain, it's the same dang thing. Your immune system, circadian rhythms controlling your sleep cycle, your metabolism, your emotional state, and your mental capacity all begin to suffer. Then if you're not sleeping well or you get sick or you begin fighting more with your partner, it adds to the guilt, the pressure, the chaos of your life. Even when something isn't a real threat, your body has no idea. It's like the Zen author Natalie Goldberg says, "Stress is an ignorant state. It believes everything is an emergency."

This long-term pressure on your physiology can leave you vulnerable to illness, disrupt your sleep patterns, increase inflammation, impair your memory, and leave you super grouchy. But before you throw in the proverbial towel and hit the freezers for some more Ben & Jerry's, I'm here to tell you how you can outsmart your wiring and live a life (relatively) free of anxiety and worry. You can be unflustered. You can survive, thrive, and live a fun and exciting life—yes, even as a busy mom.

How This Book Came to Be

In March 2020, I awoke one morning on the sofa in my office. My hips had been bothering me so much at night that I kept waking my husband, so I'd started sleeping on the sofa. I'd wake up early and do a quiet breathing meditation. You may remember back in March 2020, the planet seemed to be spiraling. My family, along with the rest of humanity, found ourselves in quarantine, hiding out from the unknown threat called COVID-19. People were worried and upset. Scared. Politics surged to the forefront of every conversation. Suspicion, fear, and outrage exploded everywhere. Racial tension mounted. Protests began in many cities, riots in others. The planet was getting, well, much more *complicated* than I'd ever seen before. On this shared planet, we became very polarized in our thoughts and opinions.

So many people I knew felt angry and appalled. The conflict and violence and turmoil seemed to become louder and louder each day as we all faced this unknown threat together. Well, actually we didn't face it "together" at all. We split. We broke apart. Fault lines spidered across families. Corporate teams, friendships, churches, and communities cracked and broke apart into two sides. One side was screaming, "This virus is a real threat, and we need to protect ourselves and others!" The other, "This virus is not as harmful as the economic damage our reaction to it is going to cause!" Both groups were feeling anger or pity for the other "ignorant" or "misled" or "duped" group. Lifelong friendships were suddenly questioned. Most adults in this generation had never experienced any global threat or challenge like this. We were all out of our depths. And it wasn't a pretty sight.

I came out of my meditation on that March morning and grabbed some paper and a pen. It all spilled out of me quicker than I could get it down on paper. For pages upon pages, I wrote about fear and anxiety. I wrote about uncertainty and basic human needs. I wrote about survival instincts and collective crises. I recalled my college psychology courses and Abraham Maslow, whose well-known theory described five fundamental human needs. He proposed a pyramid. From bottom to top it listed a hierarchy: physical needs, security, social needs, esteem, and then self-actualization. Depending on where you were in terms of need fulfillment, he posited that you'd be motivated by different things than someone who fell elsewhere in the pyramid.

I considered frameworks like the five love languages, where once you understand your own language, you're better able to communicate your needs more clearly. And once you understand your partner's or your child's language, you're able to better meet their needs and show them love. Most important, you're more likely to have compassion for yourself and compassion for others when you appreciate where they're coming from. When you understand what's driving someone else, what their core needs are, maybe you can listen with an open heart. At the time, I saw a planet where people were either so scared or so angry that they could no longer access basic human compassion. Patience and curiosity were replaced with utter shock and painful feelings of frustration. Friendships crumbled. Families cracked under the pressure. And many couples became either closer or more divided. Disbelief abounded. How could he really feel that way? How could she post *that*? How could they *support* that candidate? Do they really believe that?

As I wrote in a semi-meditative state, an idea solidified out of the ether. What if the reason for all this confusion and shock was this: Yes, we are all scared right now. The key is, we are scared of different things. We have different core drivers. We flourish in different environments. Some of us need security, some need love, some need achievements, some need a dream, and some need challenges. Depending on what we focus on most, we come to different conclusions. Different perspectives. Our fears and our values influence our perceptions. They influence our priorities and our choices. What if, like love languages and need hierarchies, there was a framework for what drives us? What if, by understanding what we value most, we were able to feel more compassion both for ourselves and for others? What if we understood that not everyone is anxious about the same things? What if we could see what our brother or neighbor or best friend was most driven by? Could we better understand why they behave or speak the way they do? What if we considered that the words and actions of others might not come from evil intentions or ignorance? What if, for many situations, it boils down to the fact that they are functioning from a different set of core values? What if what causes them to flourish is different from what drives us to flourish? What if we all have different *flourish types*?

Looking at human need psychology, I realized that if people have an unmet need in a certain area, that could contribute to the development of a particular anxiety style. Learning to harness that anxiety style can allow you to flourish instead of fluster in the face of your anxiety triggers. While Maslow's hierarchy of needs is, well, hierarchical, none of the flourish types is "higher" or "more evolved" than any other type. You likely have one primary anxiety style that can be turned into a flourish type, and one or two secondaries. What if understanding your anxiety style allowed you to better understand yourself and communicate your needs and priorities better? What if it also allowed you to have compassion for those whose actions and words made no sense to you? What if we all understood what to do and say to help ourselves feel less flustered? How could that make us feel better? More confident? More calm? More clear? Could understanding how to reach your flourish type allow you to clear the path to replace conflict with compassion? Replace frustration with patience? Disbelief with understanding? Rigidity with flexibility? Anger with wisdom? Hate with love? Fear with clarity? Sadness with joy? Would this new view of others and the world reduce the threats you perceive?

I believe it can. I believe that understanding your anxiety style and flourish type will help you feel less flustered and more confident and happy in your life. In the following pages you'll learn about the five styles. You'll see yourself, your childhood, your triggers, and your talents in the chapters that lie ahead. Together, we'll uncover your primary anxiety style and identify where it's helping in your life and where it's no longer serving you. Then we'll create a plan with specific, practical strategies you can realistically implement into your busy life and turn it into a flourish type. You'll create a toolbox of tactics that will help you feel less flustered, be more connected to those you love, and find the time and space to follow your joy more consistently.

Meet Our Star Moms

The first flourish type I'll describe (randomly selected and by no means better or worse than any other) is the Lover. These moms flourish when focusing on their relationships. They want to feel loved and connected to the people in their lives. Lover moms feel most alive when they feel wanted and liked by others. Lisa is the Lover mom we'll get to know intimately throughout the pages of this book. She is a single working mom with two kids, a 7-year-old daughter and a 10-year-old son. Divorced for just over three years, Lisa works from home as a copywriter. Her biggest drivers are her relationships with her friends and her extended family. Lisa's anxiety and frustrations stem mostly from feelings about her divorce and a fear of getting romantically involved with anyone new.

The second type we'll learn about is the Visionary. These moms flourish most when accomplishing their life's work, making a big, bold impact on the planet. What truly lights them up is finding and achieving their ultimate purpose in life. Victoria is our Visionary mom. Victoria is in her late 20s, newly married with a toddler. She hopes for more children but is having trouble conceiving baby number two. As an architect's apprentice, she's overwhelmed, trying to juggle her relationship, her budding career, and a spirited two-year-old.

Our third type is the Dynamo. These moms flourish when they're in action and feel acknowledged for their accomplishments. Appreciation and achievements make them feel alive and refuel them emotionally. The Dynamo mom wants most to feel heard, seen, and admired by those she loves and respects. Daisy, our Dynamo mom, has two children from her second marriage. She works in finance and loves checking items off her to-do list. One of her biggest fears is failure, or even seeming like a failure to those she loves and respects.

The fourth type we'll explore is the Executive. These moms flourish when achieving a level of safety and stability for themselves and their families. Executive moms are very good at planning, organizing, and managing amid the chaos of motherhood. Elizabeth is our Executive mom. She's a mom of twin boys, a part-time yoga instructor, newly turned vegan, and pretty much on her own as a parent. While her husband technically lives at home, he's gone a lot for work (and somehow gone even more when he's home). Elizabeth is most alive and thriving when she feels emotionally safe and secure; insecurity makes her anxious. Her ability to be consistent and structured helps her feel less anxious and flustered.

Our last, but not least, type is the Fighter. These moms flourish when they are fighting battles and surviving challenges. The Fighter mom is focused most on saving and protecting others. The enemy might be another person, a group, an illness, or even an environmental problem. Faith is our Fighter mom. She has four children, two in college and two teenagers still living at home. Faith is newly divorced from her childhood sweetheart. Her ability to thrive amid chaos benefited her a lot while raising her four children. Though, as her house becomes quieter and emptier, she's feeling unsettled and—you guessed it—flustered.

Each of these moms has core needs, unique superpowers, and emotional triggers particular to their flourish type. In the coming pages, you'll learn how your type is serving you and how it might be holding you back. As you get to know Lisa, Victoria, Daisy, Elizabeth, and Faith, see if you recognize yourself in any of them. Maybe there are two who resonate with you right off the bat. Notice your reaction as you read about their strengths, their struggles, and the tools they choose as each learns how to be an unflustered mom.

What to Expect

In part I, you'll learn more about how moms are uniquely affected by anxiety and stress. You'll understand how to use your motivational style, self-awareness, and gratitude to ease your fluster and simplify your life. And we'll talk about *why* it's important that the world has more unflustered moms.

In part II, we'll dig into each anxiety style and flourish type. You'll learn how to uncover your emotional triggers, celebrate your superpowers, and dispel your faulty beliefs. You'll also get customizable tools and strategies for preventing and minimizing the various stressors in your life. These include weekly, daily, and multiday practices specific to your primary flourish type.

In part III, you'll take charge and create your own personal Emergency Emotional Support Plan (EESP). You'll learn how to notice when you've been triggered, how to communicate your needs more effectively, and how to leverage your motivational style so you can realistically implement the tactics from your toolbox when you need them.

How to Use This Book

At this point, I encourage you to take a few minutes to complete the online quiz to determine your flourish type. You can find the quiz at www.flourishquiz.com. I recommend you pick the first answer that feels right for each question. Don't think about it too much. If you're not a fan of these types of quizzes, feel free to skip it. Instead, you can use the chapters in part II to determine which style has tools that you're most likely to use and which triggers and superpowers sound most like you.

I encourage you to scribble all over this book as you read it. Circle, underline, write in the margins. Go wild. This is your personal handbook, and I'd love nothing more than to see it messy with use and engagement. Also, you may see your partner or your parents in the types as you read through part II. You might read the Dynamo clues and think, *Oh my gosh, that's totally my husband!* Take a moment and ask yourself how you can best support them now that you understand them a little bit better. Are they acknowledging and celebrating their superpowers? Do they have the tools to communicate their triggers? Once you've learned how to help yourself, you can then share strategies that might work for them when they're feeling anxious or stressed. You might to want to buy this book on Audible for your mother and then buy several paperbacks for your best friends so you can have a book club, make your EESPs together, and create an unflustered moms group. *It's totally your call.*

My biggest hope is that you use this book to transform your view of yourself. Because, as self-help icon Lisa Nichols teaches, "It's your responsibility to show the world how to treat you by the way in which you treat yourself." In the following chapters, you'll learn to acknowledge all the shiny, golden parts of your personality, to celebrate your wins and embrace your superpowers. You'll uncover how your anxiety has served, supported, and maybe even saved you on occasion. You'll better understand your personal triggers so you can replace your self-judgment with self-compassion. And, you'll create your EESP. You can use the strategies you've chosen to reduce the stress and anxiety in your daily life. Finally, you'll begin to shift your sense of self-value. Instead of your worth coming from what others might say or do or feel, it will come from deep within you.

In addition to all that, when you start to implement your anti-fluster strategies from the EESP, you'll argue less with your partner, feel less frustrated with your mother, yell less at your children, spend less time lying awake at night, and cry less in your closet. As novelist and mother Jodi Picoult says, "Anxiety's like a rocking chair. It gives you something to do, but it doesn't get you very far." You might realize right away that the noisy swarm of killer bees buzzing around is actually a group of dandelion seeds. You'll close your eyes, take a deep breath, smile, and say to yourself, *Ah yes, I remember when I was surrounded by those bees. Not anymore, my friends. Not. Any. More.*

2

THE SECRET LIFE OF MOMS

REMEMBER WHEN YOUR PRIMARY RESPONSIBILITIES involved keeping yourself alive and deciding what to do for spring break? Maybe your biggest worries were finding a date for your sister's wedding and looking for an apartment with a working heater. Or, perhaps you had far larger concerns, but I'm guessing only a few of them were life-or-death situations. Then, suddenly or not so suddenly, planned or not, happy about it or not, you found yourself pregnant. The responsibility shifted. It grew.

There's a baby now, and you're in charge.

Suddenly what you eat, the baby eats. What you drink, the baby drinks. Your actions and decisions and behaviors no longer affect *just* you. Seemingly, like magic, this tiny pea will grow into a person, and you know you'll be 100 percent responsible for keeping it alive for the rest of your life (well, kinda).

Then you *gestate*. Such an innocuous word for growing an actual three-dimensional human. The baby gains 8 pounds and you gain 48. Doctors say you're not exercising enough or your blood pressure is too high. Weird blue lines spread across your skin, suggesting your body may literally split at the seams. You might experience complications or just *imagine* the many possible complications. Either way, in the end, you get to birth the baby. Now, talk about a situation where your plans and expectations seldom match reality! You hear a million birth stories about impossibly horrible things—and at most, only one or two of them actually come true.

Yes, the delivery . . . where a bunch of the stuff you *do* expect doesn't happen and stuff you *don't* expect *does* happen. The ultimate WTF? And whatever your expectations, whatever your feelings about your birthing experience, your entire life shifts as a result. For some moms, that shift feels instantaneous. For others, it seeps in through the cracks gradually. This little macadamia nut you've made into a person is now *outside* your body. I realize that's obvious. But let's take a flippin' moment here to consider that more seriously. You made a human. It took *months*. It was *inside* your body. And now, you are in a hospital bed (or somewhere, hopefully resting). And your baby is over *there*. It's lying in a plastic bin on wheels, burritoed up in a blanket *outside* your body.

You think that's mind-blowing? Well, here's the biggest change: Suddenly, meeting *your body's* needs no longer automatically results in meeting your baby's needs. Keeping *yourself* safe, warm, happy, and healthy does not ensure the baby will remain safe, warm, happy, and healthy. Nope. In fact, it often feels like you have to choose—

Baby? Or me?

In most cases, the answer is simple, right? You just spent an awful lot of time and effort making this beautiful, tiny, helpless thing. Plus, you're flooded with that special type of love—or hormones and exhaustion—that dreamily suggests you will of course always choose the baby. You innately decide that keeping your child alive is your highest priority. You're prepared to attack anyone who threatens your child's livelihood—even if that "anyone" is *you*.

Wait, what?

You have a mission: keep this small human alive. But you also have a problem: keeping your baby safe may, in fact, end up doing *you* harm— be that physically, mentally, emotionally, or all three.

It's OK. Breathe. We're gonna get through this, I promise.

This is when anxiety and uncertainty often creep in (if they haven't already set up shop in your living room). Legit worries. Ridiculous worries. Big fears. Little fears. There's so much variety, it's like a fear buffet in Vegas. But how do you know what is big or little, real or unreal? How do you know if it's a killer bee swarm or hundreds of dandelion seeds in the wind? As new moms, we can fall deeply into an abyss of physical exhaustion, emotional isolation, self-doubt, mental confusion, and severe irritability. Throw in the physiological havoc caused by your new and improved mom worries, and you certainly can't expect yourself to make decisions with any sort of clarity. Trying to function on a daily basis becomes a full-time job—except in *this* job, your boss wakes you up every 90 minutes to play or eat or poop.

The overwhelm shows up in unexpected ways. It peeks at you from the shadows. It slithers over from behind the sink. And sometimes it jumps out and smacks you right in the face. More often than not, you're utterly unprepared for this development. And because you're busy, emotionally rocked, and sleep deprived—a special combo of challenges that can, in fact, last for years—you suddenly have far fewer internal resources to help yourself.

"One of the great myths of our society is that when women are left with small children, they are not alone. The truth is that a mother left with babies is far more alone than she would be without them; every bit of energy, attention, protectiveness and care she might use to meet her own needs must first be directed toward the needs of her children . . . a woman alone can run, fight or hide, but a woman with babies is toast."
—Dr. Martha Beck

When Daisy, our Dynamo mom, first became a mother, she struggled with mild postpartum depression and felt frustrated with the weight she'd gained. She felt disconnected from her husband and couldn't help but pull away from everyone around her. She was exhausted and felt sad almost all the time. When she went back to her job, she began to feel better (and even began to feel like her body was her own again) but then felt guilty about being away from her little one every day.

Victoria, our Visionary mom, fared a little better during her passage into motherhood. A young mom, she made the transition rather smoothly. Unfortunately, she now experiences anxiety from not being able to conceive again. She feels unsupported and misunderstood because she feels like people around her think she should be grateful for her toddler and focus on that instead of a second baby. Victoria cannot stop her feelings of frustration and despair, though. Now, not only is she sad about not being able to conceive, but also she feels guilty for feeling sad about it.

Lisa, our Lover mom, took to motherhood quite easily. She had supportive loved ones around her, and both babies slept well, allowing her to recover and take care of herself more easily. Her overwhelm didn't really pop up until the kids were older and her husband announced, seemingly out of the blue, that he didn't want to be a dad or husband anymore. He left the family. As someone whose number-one priority is feeling wanted and loved by others, this was a huge hit for Lisa. It hollowed her out like an empty nutshell.

In Elizabeth's case, our Executive mom's identical twins were a total surprise. She immediately called upon her organizational skills and laid out very clear schedules for feeding and sleeping. Having her lists and keeping all the baby supplies organized kept her from feeling too overwhelmed. Unfortunately, while this helped keep Elizabeth from feeling like she was drowning, her husband perceived it as very militant and cold. He missed the loving, soft, easygoing woman he'd married, and he didn't feel connected to, attracted to, or respected by the woman he'd seen her turn into. She fell into survival mode, but it took a toll on her relationship, and now her husband is either working or busy on projects around the house, trying to stay out of her way. Although they live together, it feels more like they're roommates and business partners. For this, Elizabeth feels angry, sad, guilty, and bitter.

Faith, our Fighter mom, has four children. She got lots of support from her big family when the kids were small. Her entrance to motherhood was fraught with the typical exhaustion and frustrations. But, overall, it was a smooth transition and she kind of enjoyed the challenge of it all. Since her kids are older now, most of Faith's overwhelm stems from political and social unrest around the world. She finds herself easily upset, staying up late reading article after article about social justice issues in faraway lands.

Sorting Through the Absurdity

The big question for flustered moms: how, in a state of exhaustion, uncertainty, and worry, do moms quickly and easily tell the difference between legitimate and illegitimate threats? Because of the sheer number of changes in pregnancy, birth, and parenting, our worries stretch broad and wide. Some are legit and require our time, energy, and focus. But most of the worries we carry around *do not* merit even an ounce of our attention. Most of them, in fact, are completely absurd. Unfortunately, it's up to you—exhausted, emotional you—to sort through them and decide what makes sense for you. Uh-oh.

Running around through life with all these worries is like running through the jungle on a dark, misty night with a blindfold over your eyes . . . in flip-flops. In the gloom, everything looks scary.

That jaguar over there? It's a tree.

That urgent e-mail from the IRS? It's a scam.

That heart attack you're having? It's actually heartburn. Remember that spicy burrito you scarfed down at lunch.

So now what? You survive. You thrive. Or both. Or neither. It's different day by day—even moment by moment.

As a new mom, you feed the baby. *Then you eat an entire pint of chocolate fudge brownie ice cream.* You put the baby down for a nap. *Then you scroll through Instagram posts of new moms who look as if they ate a tapeworm and do 5,000 crunches a day.* You feel so disconnected from other adult humans that you binge-watch *Friends* reruns just for company.

Now, here comes the fun part: the advice. It's all over the place. Am I right? Books and nurses, neighbors and friends, in-laws, even strangers—everyone has a piece of advice for you. And every piece of advice takes a chunk of your confidence with it. Most of it is well-intended. *Probably.* Most of it makes a lot of sense when you first hear it. But the lack of sleep and the blizzard of responsibilities fighting for your attention make it difficult to know for sure.

What is right? Who do I trust? What feels good to me? What is best for my baby?

This, my friend, is the delicate seesaw between fear and certainty. Between confusion and clarity. Between feeling flustered and feeling calm and confident. Unfortunately, if you're anything like me, that balance between worry and confidence continues to threaten your sanity and well-being—and if left unattended, it will continue to do so, even when your kids grow up. The constant low-grade stressors cloud your ability to trust yourself. It's tougher than ever to listen to your gut, to think clearly and rationally. Instead, you slog through, manage, survive; you run and run just to keep up with the treadmill, rarely stopping to think, breathe, or refuel yourself mentally or emotionally. Maybe you're afraid that if you stop, everything you care about just might crumble into tiny pieces.

There is a way to smash those unhelpful and irrational worries. You *can* wipe them away and clear the path for clarity, for calm, for confidence.

This is what you're here to learn. It's why you've come to this exact spot at this very moment. You deserve calm. You deserve to feel confident. You deserve to have a well-functioning immune system, an efficient metabolism, clear thoughts, and great sleep. And guess what? Your child deserves a healthy, happy momma too.

When moms function from a place of confidence, clarity, and calm, they can raise children who are secure and well-balanced humans. And, those children are more likely to become the compassionate, creative, kind, communicative problem-solvers of tomorrow. But it just won't happen if Mom is constantly flustered and not taking care of herself emotionally.

The Biology of the Fluster

Anxiety shows up in our lives in a different way for each of us. We're flustered by different situations, and we become unflustered in different ways. We're all unique, right? We have different values, personalities, lifestyles, priorities, and family dynamics. It follows that different situations and challenges are going to affect us differently. We will perceive them differently. We will react to them differently. And, we will recover from them differently.

This is why the five anxiety styles and flourish types framework is so powerful. You deserve your own set of flourish tools to move in the direction of confidence, clarity, and certainty. When you dismantle the unhelpful or irrational worries of your anxiety style, you release buckets of anxiety, guilt, and self-doubt. You stop bullying yourself. With those excess worries gone, clarity and confidence can flourish. You'll feel lighter, calmer, more patient, and more capable of dealing with whatever life hands you—which, since you're a mom, is bound to be quite a lot.

I know we talked about the hormonal and chemical effects of chronic, low-grade stress. But here I want to highlight what it means for you today, in this moment. There's a whole set of factors, ranging from the biological to the practical, associated with motherhood that amplify the effects of chronic worry. The weeks or months spent in even a mild state of chronic stress affect your immune system, your metabolism, your quality of sleep, and, of course, your mood. And seriously, if you could fix those four areas (immune system, metabolism, sleep, and mood), imagine how that could totally change your life.

For one thing, having a baby has been linked to increased amygdala response in the brain, meaning that sense of heightened alertness you experience isn't random—it's part of your biological design. Humans' evolutionary biology is changing all the time, but it isn't necessarily up-to-date. As far as your body is concerned, you're not that far from a cavewoman—even if your problems are very far from cavewoman problems. Your body is still, to some degree, living as if it's up to you (and only you!) to have an intact cave, to protect that little one from the elements, to save him from a bear if necessary.

The amygdala doesn't quite get it that for most of us, there isn't actual life-or-death danger. For instance, you probably can turn on the heater if your baby is cold, as opposed to starting a fire in your cave. Even if you live in the Everglades, it's highly unlikely a crocodile is about to climb in through the bedroom window. Does the amygdala care? Nope. Its job is to be ready, and it is *not slacking on that*. So it does its thing anyway, starting a chain of events throughout your body that is hard to interrupt. We all know that feeling, right? You're late for a meeting, cannot find your keys, and then you trip and spill your hot coffee all over your pants. *Argh!*

When your amygdala freaks out and your body spikes with adrenaline and cortisol, preparing itself for a fight or flight, your metabolic system slows down. All the focus is directed toward your heart and muscles in case you need to wrestle that crocodile or run to a neighboring cave for help. So if the modern-day you wants your metabolism to work efficiently, learning how to move from a stressful state to a calm state will change your life.

Guess what cortisol also regulates? Yep, your immune system. Good thing you don't care about getting sick or feeling trim and healthy anytime soon! (Insert sarcastic eye-roll here.) It's one thing if your child is sick and you're caring for her. But what happens when *you're* sick? You get to lie in bed and someone waits on you hand and foot for a few days, right? (Only if you live in a magical place called *Neverhappens Land.*) Yes, I too used to imagine spraining my ankle or getting just sick enough to require a few days of bed rest (or even—*gasp*—hospitalization). In my dream world, this would be a lovely time. I'd sleep, and someone would bring me chicken soup and chamomile tea all day. Yeah, that never happened. If you want your immune system functioning at full capacity, you'll want to learn how to move from a fluster to a calm more easily. We'll get to *the how* in a bit, I promise.

I've mentioned that sleep deprivation often accompanies motherhood, especially early on, but I want to point out that quality of sleep matters too. I don't think there's a mom on the planet who routinely sleeps well. Awesome job, overactive amygdala! Way to prevent a bee attack! But, as we've discussed, in most cases *they are actually dandelion seeds.* Your modern-day kids are likely sleeping in real beds, in warm bedrooms, in fire-resistant pajamas. That means if you want to fall asleep more easily, actually sleep through the night, and wake up feeling alert and refreshed, you'll want to know how to shift your physiology from fear mode to calm mode.

Do you know what those spikes of adrenaline and cortisol also mess with? Your ability to concentrate, remember stuff, focus on something important, and use your brain to solve problems. Plus, there's oxytocin, that snuggly, feel-good hormone that makes you cry during sappy commercials. It's in full force when you have a baby, perhaps to convince you to continue taking care of your offspring instead of, you know, taking care of *yourself*. But the delightful oxytocin also interferes with the formation of memory. That means—bingo!—it's pretty common to start forgetting everything all the time. And that sense of forgetfulness just causes more frustration and anxiety.

When we put it all together, we're left with an indispensable truth: that thing we commonly refer to as "mommy brain" is truly nothing more than the cumulative physiological impact of chronic low-grade stress and lack of proper sleep. It's *real*. You're normal. It was a necessary part of being a mom at the beginning. But now, maybe it's time to reset, to learn some new and healthier ways to function. And while you cannot de-mommy yourself to get your pre-mommy brain back, you *can* learn to release your worries and feel less flustered. You can better manage the common stressors of life and regain a sense of control. You can eliminate that swarm of anxiety bees and finally see and think clearly again.

In other words, you can't stop your amygdala, but you can short-circuit it to better manage its effect. I like to think of this as *outsmarting stress*.

How to Outsmart Your Stress

No one likes feeling stressed out unnecessarily. I don't think I need to convince you that spending your limited time and energy fretting about moot fears is a waste. But in case this argument needs a little extra sauce, let's look at how outsmarting at least *some* of your stressors will make you not only a chiller person, but also a better mom.

You deserve to feel calm and happy. Addressing stress is really important for your own physical and mental health. But it's also good for your kids. When stress goes unchecked, irritability shifts more easily into anger, frustration into overwhelm, sadness into hopelessness, and worry into anxiety (or even panic).

The truth is that letting go of your fears—or at least those unnecessary fears—has the potential to give you so much more of what you want in your relationship with your kids. Letting go of the irritability can make space for feelings of connectedness, bonding, and love. Letting go of the frustration can make space for patience and clarity. Letting go of the sadness can make space for excitement and joy. And letting go of the worry can make space for confidence and calm.

In case you're not already convinced it's worth learning how to move from stress to calm, there's more. Aside from affecting your body, your mind, your emotions, and your relationships, stress also affects your beliefs, your thoughts, your actions, and your words. The wrong words can royally damage a relationship. A simple shift in words can also become the catalyst for a 180-degree change in your relationship with a partner, with your children, and even with yourself. It starts with changing your most basic beliefs about your overwhelm, shifting you from a disempowered state where fear is in charge to an empowered state where what once frightened you becomes your superpower.

Don't know what I'm talking about? Dream with me for a moment. Picture each of us humans as a tree. Our words and actions bloom like flowers and leaves from the branches of our tree. Our branches are made up of our thoughts. Those thought branches grow out of our trunk. And our trunk is fed from our beliefs, the roots of our tree. So it goes from roots to trunk, then branches out to the leaves and flowers. Beliefs to thoughts, then to words and actions. Our roots feed us, fuel us, and keep us from floating around in the winds. Our roots require sustenance, though—healthy soil and clean water. What feeds our roots? What sustains us? Safety, love, dreams, rest, connection. And, like a real tree, healthy food and clean water. But what if our roots aren't absorbing enough nourishment to sustain our tree? What if we don't have support, sleep, or healthy relationships? What if we're planted somewhere in unhealthy soil with not enough water? What if our roots are keeping us stuck and starved, not really allowing us to grow or thrive? Can we change them? How can we change our very roots—the source of sustenance that feeds our beliefs, thoughts, words, and actions?

For most of us, the idea of uprooting ourselves is horrifying. We rightly fear that doing it might just kill us. But I suggest there is another option, one that is found in the roots of a tree that lives deep in the Amazon rainforest. This is a special kind of tree called a *cashapona*, sort of an Amazonian jungle palm. Like many trees, the cashapona has evolved to meet its specific circumstances. It has learned to shift what isn't working, *right down to its very roots.* This tree has stilted roots that allow it to "walk." The cashapona throws out new roots in the direction of safety or better soil, building a new root system to replace the old one. Then the old roots wither and die. It continues this process until it arrives at a new foundation where it can thrive again.

To outsmart your stress, you're going to become a cashapona. And I promise you that you can. You can grow new roots. You can create new beliefs and allow the old ones to wither and die. You have this superpower. You can shift to a place where you too can thrive. You can learn how to fill yourself with the sustenance you need to truly flourish.

"Watch your thoughts, they become your words; watch your words, they become your actions; watch your actions, they become your habits; watch your habits, they become your character; watch your character, it becomes your destiny."
—Aphorism popularized by Frank Outlaw, 1977

The New Roots

To review the most important takeaways here (in case you haven't fin-ished your coffee), the multitude of mom worries causing chronic stress on your system is *no bueno*, you cannot escape to *Neverhappens Land*, and you're a cashapona. Got it?

What do you do about the fear buffet then? That, my friend, is the million-dollar question. Remember, we all have different core values, anxiety styles, and flourish types that develop in our lives. In the pages that follow, you're going to learn how to outsmart your overwhelm. You'll understand *what* your anxiety style is, *why* it developed, and *how* it has served you as a flourish type. Then you'll be able to release the parts that no longer serve you and uncover the superpowers you don't even realize lie beneath. Doing so has a very real, practical effect: armed with this new insight, you'll be able to make lasting improvements to yourself, your life, and your family.

We'll start with uncovering your anxiety style. You can skip straight to it if you think you already know which one it is; if you're not sure, or the idea of reading a book out of order wigs you out, just turn the page and keep going. Remember, unlike Maslow's hierarchy, there is no pyramid here. None of the types is better or worse than any other. You may, in fact, identify with a few of them. The point is to find the insights and tools that *most* resonate with you. This is the part where the jungle mist evaporates and you can see more clearly. Eventually, you'll be able to perceive and understand threats with more clarity and better understanding. The end result? Fewer emotional ups and downs, more patience, less frustration, and more joy—flourishing. How does that sound?

By understanding your anxiety style and flourish type, you'll be able to better understand your initial emotional reaction and feel less self-judgment and guilt. You'll be able to communicate your needs more effectively to your children and your partner. You'll be able to find the strategies that work best to reduce feelings of stress and overwhelm in your daily life. And you'll be able to better align your limited time, energy, resources, and attention with what is truly important to you, with what most fuels you and feeds your spirit. You'll go from flustered to flourishing.

3

SOCKS AND SHOES

WHAT IF YOU LEARN ALL ABOUT YOUR FLOURISH TYPE and identify all
the tools most likely to help you, but you can't actually implement them
when you need them? I get it. Sometimes, *even if* you know what will
help, you can't get yourself to do anything about it. Don't fret; I'm going
to make this a lot easier for you. You're going to grab your map, put on
your socks, and lace up your most comfortable shoes before you begin
this journey. Even with a hat, a compass, and all the snacks you can carry,
you've gotta put on your socks and shoes first. For our purposes today,
your "map" is understanding your motivational style, your "socks" are
self-awareness strategies, and your "shoes" are self-kindness. Once you
know your unique motivational style, become self-aware, and exchange
self-judgment for self-kindness, you'll be far more likely to benefit from
what you'll learn in this book.

Forcing yourself into doing the things you know are healthy and
good for you only works temporarily, if at all. Then, if or when you
fail, you feel even less motivated than when you first began. When you
understand your unique motivational style, it's as if someone cleared
your path through the jungle with a giant machete, brought you a
flashlight, and patted your brow with a cool cloth. It's so much easier.
Not only will achieving your goals and implementing your new habits
become easier, but you also might have fun while you're doing it.

What's Your Motivational Style?

Everyone has different motivational strategies that work best for them. Let's hack into *your* brain and dig into your past to unearth which motivational strategy is most likely to work for you. If you're not sure, ask yourself in what period of your life were you really, really productive. When did you feel most invigorated and excited? When did you accomplish something that was really hard? What worked for you then?

What do you do in your social life or in your career that works well for you and could be applied to your personal life? Maybe you feel very confident and in control when it comes to your body. You know that when you avoid carbs and cheese, you feel and look fabulous. You also know that you feel best when you walk every morning and go to your favorite hot yoga class twice a week. Or, maybe the opposite is true (veggie pizzas and ice baths?). Either way, it's all about you—not what works for your mother-in-law, your neighbor, or your best friend from college.

Look through the following list and circle the strategies that are most motivating for you. In other words, utilizing these tactics will make you: (1) more likely to follow through, (2) have more fun, and (3) feel the least amount of frustration and fluster.

I work best when I have an accountability partner.
I work best when I'm part of a group.
I work best when I'm on my own.
I work best when I make a financial commitment.
I work best when using micro-goals.
I work best when I'm going after a big, audacious goal.
I work best when I put it all in my calendar.
I work best when I use reminders and set alarms.
I work best when I have a deadline (otherwise, I'll procrastinate).
I work best when I give myself fun little rewards.
I work best with a strict schedule, guidelines, and consistency.
I work best with flexibility and lots of change.

For instance, I like working on my own, prefer big projects, and enjoy a flexible schedule. Others might love repetition, consistency, and an accountability partner. Some people find they work really well under deadlines and procrastinate endlessly if they have "too much time" before a task has to be completed. Some know they work really well when breaking their larger goal into bite-sized pieces and doing a bit each day (micro-goals). Still others find they work best on a team or with an accountability partner.

Let's check in with our mom stars. How do they utilize their motivational style to clear the obstacles in their jungle path? Lisa tends to follow through with her goals when she asks her best friend to be her accountability partner. Faith loves small rewards, like a croissant and a latte. Elizabeth finds she's most motivated when she reminds herself how her goals will benefit her kids' lives. Victoria prefers big, audacious goals to get herself motivated and energized. Daisy finds she works best with a deadline. Otherwise, she'll inevitably put it off and never even get around to starting.

Let's take the antianxiety self-care strategy of meditation as an example. If you want to begin a meditation practice, here are a few simple, yet powerful, motivational tactics:

Implement the new habit early in your day. Most people have the highest levels of energy, clearest mental state, and most self-control in the first half of their day. In the afternoon and evenings, it goes downhill. A complex combination of factors coalesces later in the day. Dehydration, hunger, fatigue, and stress conspire to leave you more distracted and less motivated to do whatever you had originally planned that morning. Instead of fighting this or beating yourself up about it, plan ahead. Implement your new strategy earlier in your day. Not only will you be more likely to actually do it, but also the benefits of your new habit (morning meditation) will actually help with the distraction, stress, and mood factors that pop up in the late afternoon.

For example, when I turned 40, I began a morning meditation practice. As soon as the first speckles of conscious thought began in the morning, I'd prop myself up against my headboard with my eyes still closed. I wouldn't check my phone, look in on the kids, or even use the restroom. I'd just sit up and start a simple box breathing meditation.

Four counts inhale. Four counts holding. Four counts exhale. Four counts holding again. If my mind began to race, I'd do one of two things. First, I'd try adding the Ho'oponopono mantra, which is a simple set of four phrases made popular by author and speaker Joe Vitale: *I love you. I'm sorry. Please forgive me. Thank you.* If my mind filled with something important, I'd quickly jot it down on the notepad beside my bed. Then I'd immediately return to the box breathing. I rarely need the notepad now; I trust myself to be able to access the idea later since my mind is no longer as flustered as it was at that time in my life.

Prep yourself the night before. You might find and "favorite" the guided meditation you want to do, set a reminder in your phone, and let your kids know you're doing a "calm-mommy break" before breakfast. Tell them zero interruptions unless someone's bleeding or actively vomiting. (And the bleeding should be substantial enough to merit an interruption— otherwise, it can wait. It's not like you're going to be doing a two-hour meditation right off the bat!) If you know that outside noises will distract you, have a white noise machine or earplugs nearby. If you know you'll feel chilly, place a cozy sweater on your bedside table. If you know your husband will get on his phone and start talking back to his notifications first thing in the morning, ask him if he can do it in the kitchen instead.

For instance, I always have a mug of water next to my bed and ear- plugs under my pillow. If I know that I'm more likely to have 10 minutes to myself a bit later in the morning, I'll make my coffee, then walk down the street to a nearby park and do my meditation there on a bench once everyone in my house is set on their morning classes. (Yes, we are homeschooling at the time of this writing.) The folks walking their dogs at the park look at me a bit strangely, but I'm pretty sure they're just jealous.

Tell someone else you're going to do it. Do you have a sister who medi- tates, a coworker, or a friend from college? Often, you'll let *yourself* down before you'll let *someone else* down. Use this to your advantage. Tell your meditating friend that you want to start a morning meditation practice. Ask them about the benefits they've seen in their life. Then tell them you'd like an accountability partner to help you get this practice ingrained in your day more easily. Maybe shoot them a meditating yogi emoji every morning that you successfully attempt a meditation. If you don't have a friend in mind, you can use a meditation app where you can click a daily box and celebrate completing your new daily meditation routine.

I like to surround myself with like-minded people. Even better, I try to surround myself with people I want to learn from. I want to grow as a result of merely being around them. I want to watch how they function in their lives. Entrepreneur and motivational speaker Jim Rohn famously said, "You are the average of the five people you spend the most time with." In fact, current social science researchers say even one person can greatly affect your behavior and choices. When you surround yourself with people whose values and practices you respect, those values and practices become a part of the conversation and routine. For instance, I recently listened to a video message from one of my dear entrepreneur mom friends, and she said she had to cut her response short because she wanted to meditate before getting ready for her next presentation. And just the day before, I was on a video call with a friend who had to jump off the call at 2:00 PM for her daily meditation with her boyfriend. What incredible reinforcement for my own meditation practice, to surround myself with people I admire and respect who are also avid meditators, right?

Start small. You're far more likely to succeed and persevere if you aim small. Try to meditate for three minutes every morning. And call it a huge success if you manage to actually do it three times that week. If you're practicing a box breathing meditation, you can start with four rounds of box breathing. Starting small works well for many people because it's a way to break through one of the most common objections: "I don't have time." The truth of the matter is, you make time for (1) what is most important to you and (2) what benefits you most. With moms, it's a bit more complicated, though. We often find time for (1) what is most important to our children, our partners, and our parents and (2) what benefits *them* most. Starting super small can help to reduce the likelihood that the "I don't have time" excuse will carry any weight. Who cannot make time for five slow, deep breaths? OK, three then. Three slow, deep breaths. Start there and see what happens.

Think of others. If that bit in the last tip resonated with you—about how moms do for others first—then listen up. Let's use that to your advantage. Think of all the ways that having a calmer, unflustered mom might help your children. Would you maybe have more patience? Would you be less likely to lose your temper or yell? Would you be more likely to be playful with them? Would you be more likely to remember that permission slip, order the birthday present, or handle the general level of noise and chaos in your home?

For instance, whenever I start to talk myself out of taking time to meditate (I now meditate every morning and every night), I remember the benefits to my family at large. They love, love, love it when I am silly and light. They see me stressed and worried, and it stresses and worries them. They see me flustered, and it flusters them. They hear me yell, then they yell at each other. So often, on a day that seems like everyone is at one another's throats, I can scan back and see that my mood often was the catalyst. I skipped a meditation or some other form of proper self-care, and ended up tornadoing into the day, already agitated and irritated with the world. There is zero doubt in my mind that every minute I spend meditating benefits my children, my husband, and my relationship with all five of them immensely.

Link the new habit to something you already do regularly. The author of *Tiny Habits*, Dr. B. J. Fogg, recommends linking a new habit to an activity you already do every day. You can link it to something you do at the same time of the day you want to do the new habit, in the same room, or within the same "theme." For instance, if you want to start a morning meditation, you can link it to making your bed in the morning (time of day and location) or link it to another wellness practice you already do, like working out or drinking green juice.

When I began my morning meditation practice, I linked it to waking up in the morning. Other options include doing a short meditation while you make your morning coffee, take a shower, or simply pull your car to the side of the road after you drop off the kids at school. Silence your phone, turn it face-down on the seat so you're not remotely tempted, and take five slow, deep breaths. If you have more time, do a guided meditation. Gabby Bernstein has a beautiful, simple morning meditation called "Morning Mantras" that I listen to at least four times a week.

Give yourself a small reward. Nearly everyone enjoys some sort of reward. As adults, we seldom receive accolades or acknowledgment for a job well done. So much of the work we do is cyclical: The laundry is never "finished" because we're constantly creating new dirty laundry. The meals are never "done" because everyone will have to eat again in three hours. So much of what we do as mothers involves temporary "wins" despite the fact that our job lasts 18 years minimum. This is why I highly recommend giving yourself a small reward. Before you jump to chocolate (which is totally what I would do), I suggest you choose something that leaves you with a more enduring joy. In chapter 9, you'll learn about the difference between surface self-care and true self-care. In the meantime, every day you successfully meditate for five minutes, give yourself five extra minutes in the shower or make a phone date with a girlfriend or jam out to your favorite old-school hip-hop song.

I believe you'll find, especially if your new habit is a morning medi-tation, that the benefits of meditating soon become powerful motivators in and of themselves. After meditating steadily for the last seven years, I definitely cherish and protect that time, and regret when I don't manage to make space for my morning and nighttime meditations. Now, my husband (who is not a meditator, by the way) reminds me to meditate since he can see how much better I feel when I do it regularly.

Using these motivational strategies is the simplest and easiest way to start doing something new. If you try to utilize a motivational style that works for your sister (but not for you), not only is it likely to fail, but you just might find yourself feeling lousier than when you started. If you know that starting small doesn't appeal to you, don't bother doing so. If you get the sense that prepping yourself the night before will make a huge difference, do that. Knowing yourself well, and using that information to set yourself up for success, is the surest and simplest way to reduce your anxiety.

Remember the Benefits

After you've identified your motivational style, shift your focus to the benefits of doing this work. How will understanding your flourish type and using the strategies within these pages change your life? How will feeling less flustered every day affect your life? How might your relationships improve? Will you feel less irritable and impatient? Will you argue less with your partner? What kind of relationships can you build instead? Could less overwhelm in your life foster more connection, compassion, communication, care, and kindness in your relationships?

How might you parent differently? Will you lose your temper less, yell less, cry less, and then feel less guilty later? Could less fluster in your life foster more confidence, patience, flexibility, calm, and understanding when dealing with your children? How will your work and career life change with stress no longer at the wheel? Will you be able to focus more, be more creative, and find more solutions to the challenges that inevitably arise? Could less overwhelm in your life benefit your income, your work relationships, and your future opportunities?

How will you feel when your head hits the pillow each night if you feel less flustered and overwhelmed each day? Calm instead of irritable? Fulfilled instead of flustered? Relaxed instead of exhausted? Happy instead of sad? Proud instead of frustrated? Sorry for all the questions here. But seriously, can you see how many important aspects of your life can benefit from reducing your stress and anxiety?

It's well worth your time to jot down the many benefits you'll enjoy when you no longer feel like you're being chased by bees and attacked by crocodiles. Look back at the preceding three paragraphs and circle the words representing what you want more of in your life. (Warning: Do not circle what you want less of, like "argue less." Instead, circle or write in the margin what you want *more* of.) Then every time you look at this page, your eyes will see those benefits highlighted. These are your goals. And you, my friend, are worthy of a life with all of them. The time, energy, and neurological chemicals you release when feeling stressed (like adrenaline and cortisol) can instead be spent in ways that *add* value and joy to your life in a deep and meaningful way.

According to one of my favorite speakers and authors, Gabby Bernstein, "Stress is actually the number one thing that blocks people from their happiness and well-being and from getting what they want." I agree with her wholeheartedly. Do you know anybody who has an incredibly blessed life, yet they complain and focus incessantly on the negative? What we focus on grows. When we only pay attention to the cracks in the asphalt, that's all we see. When we focus on the dandelions growing through those same cracks, we begin to see flowers everywhere.

Motivational Styles: The Mom Stars

Let's circle back to our mom stars. Daisy, our Dynamo mom, doesn't want to let her anxiety control her decisions anymore. She wants to feel like her value doesn't depend on doing or being or accomplishing the next thing. When folks first meet Daisy, they think she seems cold or overly practical, but once they get to know her, they see a very loyal friend with a fabulously dry sense of humor. She's hoping to reduce her fluster by balancing that internal drive for achievement with an appreciation for the present moment. Daisy really wants to slow down and connect more deeply with those she loves, to not miss out on the present because she's busy planning and organizing the next thing. She wants to use small rewards and implement new strategies early in her day. With less stress in her life, she looks forward to relaxing with a small glass of whiskey in the evenings and enjoying puzzles and board games with her family.

Victoria, our Visionary, hopes to learn how to enjoy the little things and feel content and happy in her journey to accomplish the big things. She wants to figure out how she will make an impact in the world but also enjoy her life in the meantime. She's quiet and kind and humble, yet driven and ambitious. Victoria is optimistic, but also very competitive and hard on herself. She often feels anxious about not doing what she's meant to be doing—and then she feels stressed about not even knowing what it is she's meant to be doing. She's motivated most when she links a new practice to something she's already doing. She also loves giving herself a small reward when she's successful.

Lisa, our Lover, hopes to learn how to find that balance between connecting with a romantic partner and not completely losing herself in the relationship. Her mom left the family when she was only two, leaving her grandmother as her primary caregiver, because her father worked two jobs. When Lisa's husband left her after 10 years together, it was a surprise to her. As someone who is driven by her relationships and bonds with others, she still carries a lot of self-doubt and self-judgment, often blaming herself for her husband leaving. She's motivated most by thinking of others and starting small. Lisa feels most anxious about her friendships and coworkers, constantly questioning whether they truly love her and want her in their lives.

Elizabeth, our Executive, hopes to learn from her flourish type how to reconnect with her husband and possibly save her marriage. Growing up, her father was in the US Air Force and the family moved around a lot. The constant change was a stressor for her. As an adult, Elizabeth feels most calm and secure when she can manage her environment and plan her future. She thrives in situations where she can organize and make lots of to-do lists. Changing plans last minute or dealing with flaky friends leaves her very anxious and uncomfortable. Her favorite motivational strategies include prepping the night before and remembering the benefits.

Faith, our Fighter, hopes to learn how to reduce her addiction to social media and find a different job that suits her flourish type superpowers better. When people first meet her, they see a fierce, confident woman. She makes good money as a real estate agent, but she has trouble hanging on to it. Just when things start piling up, something seems to go wrong and the money is gone again. She plans on utilizing the motivational strategies of an accountability partner and implementing those new strategies first thing in the morning if possible. Faith often finds herself anxious about finances and stressed about the state of the planet.

Becoming More Self-Aware

Just like in Alcoholics Anonymous, the first step to getting help is admitting there's a problem in the first place. If you cannot acknowledge the stress you're under or the degree of anxiety you're experiencing, it's not likely you'll get the help you need and deserve. In each chapter, we'll dig into the hallmark triggers and common clues of each anxiety type so you can develop a keen sense of self-awareness. The quicker you notice you're off, the quicker you can utilize your EESP and resolve your anxiety.

One key note about self-awareness: This is not permission to beat yourself up. Noticing your fluster is *just* that, an observation. There is no judgment involved. Why? Because judgment is (1) a waste of your precious time and (2) a way to keep you from moving forward and actually doing something about it. If you want to sit around and beat yourself up for feeling anxious, this book is not for you. If you want to complain about how flustered you are but have zero intention to make changes in your life, this book is not for you. To continue here, you're going to learn to notice your feelings and emotions *without* judgment. When you move forward from a state of self-kindness and understanding, you'll regain control of your life more easily and more quickly. Convincing yourself it's not raining outside won't make the clouds part and the sun reveal itself. Self-honesty is key.

I get it, you may not love the fact that you're feeling anxious or flustered. You may not even feel your anxiety is "justified." Whether you deny your feelings or try to discredit them altogether doesn't matter. The sooner you accept the reality of your emotional state, the sooner you can actually do something about it. As author and mother Karen Salmansohn says, "Anxiety happens when you think you have to figure out everything all at once. Breathe. You're strong. You got this. Take it day by day."

Here are a few of my favorite strategies for self-awareness and self-acceptance:

Do an inner child meditation. Search YouTube or meditation apps for a highly rated inner child meditation. This type of meditation can elicit intense emotional reactions, so don't try it when you're feeling super emotional or depressed. Inner child meditations can be deeply therapeutic. However, if you've experienced significant trauma in your life, I recommend you work with a trained therapist when doing inner child work. (This meditation can be particularly powerful for Fighter moms.)

Start a self-gratitude practice. Each night before bed, write down two specific qualities or traits you appreciate about yourself. Alternate between general qualities like "I'm a good friend" and specific traits like "I always remember to call my cousin Sarah on her birthday." The more specific you can get, the more likely you will actually believe the compliment and feel the positive emotions related to it. I recommend doing it before bedtime because going to sleep from a mental space of gratitude often helps you sleep better and wake in a more positive mood.

Ask yourself, *What would my friends say?* What do some of your closest friends and trusted family members say they like and appreciate about you? What do they come to you for help about? What do friends trust you with? Where do they most value your insight and opinions? Often, we discount our gifts because they come so naturally to us. Taking time to notice what people say about you and when they most seek you out can help you recognize and appreciate your special qualities more easily.

Make a list of mistakes in your past that you might have avoided if you had more self-awareness and self-acceptance. This is a tricky one. I do not want you to use this as an excuse to beat yourself up. What I want is for you is to find the motivation to turn your eyeballs on yourself, especially if that's something you don't typically do. Were the last six arguments you had *all* someone else's fault? If so, I challenge you to look within and see how you might have contributed. Where in your life could you have saved yourself angst and frustration if you'd been a bit more self-aware at the time? This is an area that is ever growing. You're never quite "done" being self-aware, because you're human. And as humans, we're ever changing and growing. Creating a consistent practice of checking in with yourself is a powerful way to minimize future mistakes and mishaps.

Celebrate! What problem did you *used to* have that you no longer have? Did you ever acknowledge or celebrate that win? With the amount of time mothers spend on other people and the amount of attention we give to the achievements of others, we rarely acknowledge and celebrate our own wins. I hate to say it, but if you're waiting for someone else to step up and do it, you'll likely be waiting a long, long time. Instead, plan ahead and celebrate with those who support you most. Text a college friend, "I just landed that contract I've been working on for three months!" Schedule happy hour drinks with your favorite neighbor. Make an announcement at dinner to the family and suggest a toast. Make sure to tell your family or friends how long you've been working on this goal, how much effort it took, and how much it means to you. (This can be particularly powerful for Visionary moms.)

For instance, when I published my first book, I did not wait and hope someone would make a big deal out of it. I'd read enough stories of other authors talking about how anticlimactic their "pub day" was. It's a day you know about and dream about for many months in advance. For the publication of my first book, *Stretch Marks*, I invited all my favorite people in our new hometown to our favorite restaurant. I called it a launch party. I decided to spend about the same amount of money we'd spent on one of my kids' birthday parties. The night was magical. I felt loved and appreciated and celebrated. I had to schedule it and make space for it, but it was well worth it.

Get balanced. Do you acknowledge and celebrate your wins *as much* as you punish or judge yourself for your shortcomings? How much time do you spend ignoring your needs or beating yourself up? Let me guess. Four times a day for a few minutes each time? OK, so now you owe yourself at least 12 minutes today to acknowledge and celebrate what you did well. What are you proud of? What did you handle well? What did you get done? What fires did you put out? Give yourself a giant 12-minute pat on the back. Got it? Bonus points if you spend *twice* the amount of time noticing your good qualities than your "areas of improvement." (This can be particularly powerful for Dynamo moms.)

Gracefully receive compliments. What do you say when someone says "You're so smart!" or "Your kids are amazing!" or "You look fabulous today!" Do you blow it off? Like, "Oh it's no big deal, really." Do you counter their compliment with a self-insult? Like, "Oh gosh, you should have seen me yesterday, I was a mess!" Or, do you gracefully accept the compliment by simply saying "Thank you. I really appreciate you saying that."

Try a mantra mirror practice. Take a moment in the bathroom to look into the mirror. Focus on your eyes and repeat: *You are enough. You are safe. You are worthy. You are loved.* I recommend you say whatever you most wanted or needed to hear as a child. This can feel totally awkward. It can also be an intense experience. However, it's intense because it can be deeply therapeutic. Creating a daily or weekly habit of doing this self-supportive mantra mirror practice is a wonderful way to instill self-love and self-acceptance. (This is particularly powerful for Lover moms.)

Practice a worthiness guided meditation. Several of my workshops and online programs include a guided meditation on worthiness. Self-worth lies at the heart of so many of our challenges. Often we can see this in our children more easily than we can see it in ourselves. A child who lacks self-worth might easily be swayed by others into making poor decisions. They might become a target for bullies or controlling partners. They might begin to self-medicate with drugs or alcohol or hurt themselves with cutting. Modeling healthy self-worth as a parent is a huge step in the right direction. It also creates a much higher likelihood that your children will develop healthy levels of self-worth. (This can be particularly powerful for Executive moms.)

Check in with yourself. Use an app like Vibeonix as a daily check-in for emotional intelligence. While technology can lead to distraction and stress, plenty of incredible companies have created technologies to serve and support emotional well-being. Vibeonix was created by a good friend of mine and utilizes patented voice technology to give real-time feedback to users on their emotional state. You can also use the app's journals and positive thoughts sections to improve your psychological well-being.

"Having compassion starts and ends with having compassion for all those unwanted parts of ourselves. The healing comes from letting there be room for all of this to happen: room for grief, for relief, for misery, for joy."
—Pema Chodron

Gratitude

In part III of this book, we'll dig into a smorgasbord of practical strategies for reducing anxiety and stress. But one is so incredibly important and effective that it's worth an *early* highlight—gratitude.

It's no joke. It's not a nice-to-do sort of thing. Gratitude is one of the single most powerful strategies to reduce anxiety and stress, regardless of your flourish type. The more minutes of every day you spend in a state or feeling of gratitude, the better. Gratitude increases empathy, compassion, resilience, and feelings of happiness. In terms of sleep, those who practice gratitude before bedtime find the quality and quantity of their sleep improves. Physically, gratitude improves heart rate variability and reduces systemic inflammation in your body. Studies also show reductions in feelings of jealousy, depression, stress, anger, and anxiety. One of the most inspiring transformational thought leaders, Lisa Nichols, describes gratitude as "the magnet for everything good and empowering. Fear and lack lose their power in the space of gratitude."

Why Is Gratitude So Powerful?

Practicing gratitude balances out our natural "negativity bias." We're wired to disproportionately notice our pain, our mistakes, and potential threats in our environment. Unfortunately, this natural bias toward the bad can leave us with an unbalanced and totally unrealistic version of reality. Practicing gratitude counters that natural negativity bias because it forces us to proactively notice the good stuff.

Practicing gratitude releases the feel-good brain chemicals such as dopamine and serotonin, allowing us to sleep better, think clearer, and feel more joyful.

It allows us to feel happier and more hopeful, which makes us more pleasant to be around. (Your family and friends will thank you for it!)

How to Start a Gratitude Practice

Keeping a nightly gratitude journal is an effective way to cultivate the *feeling* of gratitude. I recommend you write down one big thing and one little thing you're grateful for each night before you go to bed. Be as specific as possible.

For instance, I'm grateful I have a fridge full of food for my family and that my husband made dinner tonight so I had more time to work on my writing.

Create a "Kitchen Gratitude Jar" with some colored paper and markers so everyone in the family can note something small and specific they're grateful for throughout the week. Then, at the end of the week, the family can read the notes aloud together. There's no reason we cannot give our children the opportunity to learn with us. In fact, it can be quite powerful to admit to your children that you want to improve your emotional well-being. Imagine if they could grow up thinking it's healthy and normal to be emotionally self-aware. What if you modeled what it looks like to be committed to finding ways to better manage and respond to our various human emotional states?

Say a routine of "gratefuls" at dinnertime. This is a fabulous way to focus on the positive and reconnect as a family. I recommend making it playful and fun. This can be particularly powerful if you have multiple children and they don't always get along perfectly. Each member of the family says one compliment about the character or behavior of the family member to their left—something they appreciate or admire about that sibling or parent. For instance, "I appreciate how Jenny always gets me a Band-Aid from the cupboard when I hurt myself outside," or "I think Jenny is really creative and her elephant drawings are super cool."

When it comes to gratitude, the key is cultivating the *feeling* of gratitude in your body and heart. Merely rattling off a long list of items without actually feeling the emotion of gratitude fails to maximize the benefits. It's being in an emotional state of gratitude that leads to the benefits in your body, mind, and relationships. When starting a gratitude practice with the whole family, the sooner the better. Even if your children are toddlers, you can start a family gratitude practice. If your teens are uninterested, just start modeling it. You can tell them directly or write them notes expressing what you admire, respect, or appreciate about them.

> *What you focus on grows.*
> *What you acknowledge and express*
> *gratitude for grows even faster.*

Self-Kindness Isn't Optional

One more tip before we move on: please be kind to yourself. Bestselling author and mom Jen Hatmaker says, "Be patient. Do the best with what you know. When you know more, adjust the trajectory." None of us does everything right or has all the information we need. Life is not a game of archery. None of the happy, healthy, and wealthy moms I know experienced a straight shot at their success. They too dealt with childhood traumas, mom guilt, and constant self-questioning. They made mistakes, and they failed often. As long as you are kind to yourself, you can get up, learn from your missteps, and continue to move forward in the direction of your dreams. Life is a journey. What lessons will you learn here? How will you grow? Can you love and learn and laugh along the way?

"My dad encouraged us to fail growing up. He would ask us what we failed at that week. If we didn't have something, he would be disappointed. It changed my mindset at an early age that failure is not the outcome—failure is not trying. Don't be afraid to fail."
—Sara Blakely

It won't serve you to use the content in this book as a way to judge yourself, feel more resentful toward your parents, or shake your fist at the heavens for giving you such a crappy start in life. Yeah, I know some of us get a high from the amped-up energy of anger and frustration. Some of us actually have learned how to turn that energy into external motivation. However, if you tend to get lost in resentment and frustration, let's change that habit. It doesn't help you, and it certainly doesn't punish whoever hurt you. Instead, let's resist the urge to mentally beat up on ourselves or on anyone else. *Cashaponas simply don't have time for that!* We're far too busy growing new roots and walking to healthier spots so we can flourish. When you notice yourself becoming self-critical, be *extra* gentle and *extra* kind. Shift your focus to what serves you at this moment. Breathe deeply. Feel some gratitude. And then stay mentally in the moment, because this is when magic happens. In *this* moment—with air in your lungs, cortisol and adrenaline levels steady, and self-kindness in your heart—you can learn, understand, and grow. It's only then that everything in your life will shift. It's then that you can begin to truly flourish.

Ready? It's time to grow some new roots.

PART II

FROM
ANXIETY STYLES
TO FLOURISH TYPES

4

THE LOVER 💜

ARE YOU A LOVER MOM? LET'S FIND OUT. Getting to know your primary anxiety style and flourish type will lead to more self-acceptance and self-kindness, less conflict with those you love, and a healthy way to navigate this life. If this is your type, this chapter will allow you to better understand yourself so you can have more of what you want in your life.

Remember Lisa? She's our Lover mom. She truly values her relationships with others. One of the most important things to her is the amount of time she spends with friends and family. She values a deep emotional connection. She thrives when she feels wanted, loved, and connected with others. Lisa's anxiety flares up most when she feels unworthy, unliked, or abandoned. Women with this anxiety style may have been told they have a "fear of abandonment." Before you ask, no, you don't only develop this anxiety if you were left by the side of a road wrapped in a weathered blanket in a wicker basket on a dark and stormy night. You develop this type because of how your individual personality is intertwined with the past events and experiences in your life—regardless of whether they were traumatic or not. As it turns out, you don't actually need to *be* abandoned to *fear* being abandoned.

Lisa developed this anxiety style because early in her life she felt utterly alone and unsupported. She learned how to survive in this world without support from others and how to protect herself. She felt early on that the most important thing in life is a connection with others—feeling loved and appreciated. In a moment of perceived abandonment or unworthiness, she learned a style of interacting with the world, and today she continues to reach for it to serve and support herself. When feeling particularly flustered or anxious, Lisa's need to connect and feel love grows. As a Lover, Lisa's priorities, values, decisions, fears, perceptions, thoughts, behaviors, and beliefs are driven by the need to feel loved and wanted in this world.

The skills and talents you develop in your flourish type allow you to become an expert in the areas that are most important to you. For Lovers, it's feeling emotionally connected to and valued by others. Lisa's flourish type might be difficult for other types to understand, because it highly influences what she focuses on most. It's like a filter that translates her perceptions of the world around her. Lisa's experience of the people she meets, the challenges she faces, and the opportunities she's offered are all translated through this lens. When you're a Lover, your decisions and your emotions are fueled by a deep underlying desire to feel worthy of love, attention, and affection.

"There is nothing more satisfying than being loved for who you are and nothing more painful than being loved for who you're not but pretending to be."
—Neil Pasricha

The Lover Clues

If this is your anxiety style, you're likely to feel sad or upset when you come home to an empty house. You feel better when someone you care about is there when you arrive. When friends or family are together at an event or dinner without you, it may leave you feeling hurt or disappointed. You may need those you love to be close by in order to feel energized and productive. If your partner or friends don't respond quickly to texts or messages, you might become frustrated and upset. When those you care about are critical about your behavior or choices, you might be quick to tears or anger. You might be unable to shake off criticism that other people seem to shrug off easily.

If you're a Lover, you might hold off on sharing your real feelings for fear that friends or loved ones might pull away from you. You might wonder if people actually *like* you, second-guessing if they really want you nearby or worrying that they feel obligated to include you. You might rely heavily on family and friends for emotional support and guidance, not fully trusting yourself. It might also feel uncomfortable or even scary not knowing what others think of you. Your feelings of self-worth fluctuate depending on what other people think of you and how much time they spend with you—or, more accurately, what you *think* they think of you. Maybe you spend a lot of time and energy analyzing how others behave toward you as you attempt to figure out if they truly love you, accept you, and want you in their lives.

Sometimes, you may even feel embarrassed because you feel that your happiness relies on the actions and words of others. In relationships, you might find yourself with untrustworthy partners—partners whose words and behaviors trigger your deepest fears. Then these partners might react to your concerns with comments like "You're crazy!" or "Why do you always overreact like this?" Lisa says that if her partner texts to say he's working late, her stomach drops and her mind spirals off into worst-case scenarios. Her thoughts range from *he's lying because he's cheating* to *he's going out with friends but doesn't want me to know* to *he's staying late at work to avoid spending time with me*. The challenge is that many of Lisa's relationships did, in fact, involve men who ended up lying or cheating. She often flips back and forth between trusting her gut and questioning herself. This emotional seesaw would make anyone feel unstable, confused, and flustered.

Did any of these clues resonate with you? We often assume that most people would feel the same way we feel. If your initial response to these clues was *Well, yeah, of course, wouldn't anybody feel that way?* then this may be your anxiety style. And remember, while you may resonate most with one style, it's likely you have a secondary type too. So keep reading.

Here's the key to really knowing if you're a Lover mom: When you have these reactions, do you later feel embarrassed? Are you frustrated with your triggers, thinking others wouldn't be so bothered? Do you ever feel like you're being irrational for caring so much? Do friends, family, or partners tell you you're oversensitive, insecure, or needy? When you're like Lisa, not only are you afraid of abandonment, but you're also afraid of being abandoned for your fear of abandonment!

Let me tell you here and now, my friend: you are not crazy. In fact, you're wicked smart. Seriously. You've developed a unique skill and are highly attuned to others. You value human connection. These are all good things. There are many areas in the natural world, including plants and animals, where two species form a symbiotic relationship that helps both partners. All over the planet, there are species that function much better in a group than alone. Humans are a social species. We depend on one another physically, emotionally, and spiritually. Like all five flourish types, you've developed this style for good reason. It's allowed you to function with less anxiety in many areas of your life, and it's allowed you to focus on what you value most. Because you highly value these connections in your life, with healthy habits your relationships flourish.

That's why we are not here to change who you are. No way. Instead, let's figure out the areas of this style that serve you really well and celebrate those—help you turn fluster to flourishing. Then we'll figure out the parts of your anxiety style that no longer serve you, and we'll learn together how to release those. Last, you'll get new communication strategies to minimize your unhealthy cycles. You deserve peace and happiness. You're a Lover, baby, and that is flippin' fabulous!

The Lover Cycles

If you're still unsure about how this style applies to your life, let's touch on some common trends. You may have patterns of distrust or jealousy in your friendships or romantic relationships. You might vacillate between feeling clingy (quick to attach and wanting to be together constantly) and distant (stalling your relationships and remaining detached physically or emotionally). While in a relationship, you might have a history of either acting very controlling and judgmental or acting like you don't care at all what the other person does. This is a history of extremes—an internal fight between craving love and attention and the fear of rejection and abandonment. Finding a balance of healthy intimacy and healthy independence might feel unobtainable or even just uncomfortable.

This anxiety style might also affect your life in more subtle ways. Fear of abandonment can influence your career decisions or limit your propensity to take risks (reducing opportunities for jobs, travel, etc.). It may keep you in an unhealthy relationship for too long. It may also keep you from entering a new relationship for fear of potential abandonment. Financially, this anxiety may look like one of two extremes: difficulty planning, investing, and saving for the future, or solely saving for the future and not enjoying any money wins in the moment because you feel you cannot depend on anyone else to take care of you.

If you're a Lover like Lisa, you might also be highly self-critical. Do you have a history of blaming, shaming, or beating yourself up in general? I'm all about self-kindness—and not only because it's the *right* thing to do or a *nice* way to behave.

> *Self-kindness and self-acceptance are necessary first steps for learning or growing in any positive direction.*

If you're busy spending time and emotion beating yourself up about the past, you're not only missing out on the present, but you're also missing the opportunity to move forward in the direction of your dreams.

The Lover's Baloney Beliefs

Understanding the "baloney beliefs" underlying your anxiety style can be challenging. While reading these might sting a bit, it's an important step in this process. By bringing these uncomfortable beliefs to the surface of your conscious mind, you can release them much more easily—take the wind from their sails, so to speak. Baloney beliefs are the unsubstantiated, accidental beliefs you often don't even realize you have. Let's take a moment to uncover the baloney beliefs that are most common for your anxiety style. That way, we can start to dismantle them together. As author and philanthropist Paulo Coelho said, "Stress, anxiety and depression are caused when we are living to please others."

Remember how you're a cashapona? If your roots are no longer serving you, if they're no longer feeding you nutrient-rich soil or sufficient water, let's get you moving. You can grow strong, new roots by creating healthier beliefs that support you better.

Understanding exactly how you ended up rooted in this particular spot is less important than learning the skills to move to a healthier place. The first step, though, is knowing where you are now. Where are your roots planted? What are those unsupportive beliefs that aren't serving you well? If you're a Lover mom like Lisa, you may identify with some of these baloney beliefs:

- I am unlovable.
- I am not worthy of affection or attention.
- I have to work hard to earn love, affection, or attention from others.
- I don't feel like I can do this alone.
- People are untrustworthy.
- I am missing out.
- I am not good enough, smart enough, or lovable enough.
- I have to change myself in order to be loved.
- I have to act like a different person to be loved.

The Lover Contributors

You're probably wondering where these baloney beliefs originated. How did they take hold? How did they end up coloring so much of your life? I'll touch on a few possibilities, though I invite you not to dwell on them. In the meantime, just know they could have been a variety of experiences—huge or tiny. There's a good chance that your baloney beliefs came from the perception of parental neglect or abandonment—which, of course, could be physical, like a death or divorce, or emotional, like substance abuse or mental health problems. Your anxiety style could have stemmed from a prolonged illness of a loved one or a romantic betrayal (or a series of betrayals). Even inconsistent or conditional love from a caretaker could result in the development of a Lover anxiety style. Rejection from schoolmates, bullying, or isolation during your formative years might also result in this type.

One of the Lover types in my community, Allison, grew up as an only child with parents who constantly fought and yelled at each other. Her mother slowly began to drink more and more over the years, which ignited even more fighting and discord in the house. Allison remembers taping her school photo to the bottom of the vodka bottle her mom kept under the kitchen sink. She had hoped that her mom would see her picture and decide to choose her over the vodka. As you might have guessed, it didn't work. The vodka already had a stranglehold on her mother. When her parents finally divorced when she was 15, her father left the country with another woman he'd started dating. Allison's father had acted as her primary caregiver for much of her life—braiding her hair, making school lunches, and taking her to the mall with her friends. Allison can't recall whether he left for weeks or months. All she remembers is a deep feeling of being alone and abandoned. As an adult, she finds coming home to an empty house, particularly at night, extremely unsettling. She says that's when her parents mostly fought, in the evenings, when it was dark outside. Her mother now has over 15 years of sobriety, and the two have come together with understanding and forgiveness.

Many Lovers, like Allison, seek to fill a void of love and solitude. They want to be surrounded by people who love them. They want to know that they are a priority in the hearts of those they care about and respect. For many moms, there's a big aha moment when they uncover the single childhood experience that most contributed to their anxiety style. Once they can connect the dots and better understand themselves, it's much easier to let go of the self-judgment (or shame) and move forward.

The Lover Triggers

So now what? How do you change a lifelong anxiety style so that it no longer controls you? How do you stop those negative patterns and start new, healthier habits? Let's begin with situational triggers. These are the moments when your anxiety style is actively engaged. If you can notice a trigger while it's happening, you'll be able to more purposely *respond*, instead of *react*, to the situation.

The first step is noticing when you're being triggered. I encourage you to take a moment, right now, to identify your most common triggers. These are typical situations, people, or phrases that leave you feeling more hurt or upset than feels appropriate for the situation. As you read the list, circle the ones that particularly spark an emotional reaction in your body.

"I'm going to be late."
"Sorry, my phone was dead."
"I have to take a work trip."
"I have a new coworker."
"I'm going out with some friends."
"I have to cancel our plans."
"I just want to be alone right now."

Sometimes the same trigger that will have a minor effect on you at one point in time will have a huge effect on you at another point. Your tolerance level will almost always depend on your emotional fuel tank. Maybe you recently returned from a fantastic family vacation or your coworkers had a party for you. At this point, you're feeling very safe and loved, appreciated, and connected with the people around you. If your partner texts to say they have to work late that night, you might shrug it off as no big deal. (Your emotional tank was nice and full.) However, if you just had a huge fight with your best friend and a difficult day at work, that same text from your partner might leave you a heaping hot mess of emotion. (Your tank was low.) Allison says that she feels very anxious if her husband or a close friend says, "I need some space right now" or, "Sorry, I didn't check my phone." Luckily, she uses many of the communication strategies I share in chapter 11. Her husband now understands her triggers more deeply and accommodates her whenever he can.

Understanding and acknowledging your triggers is an important key to insight and taking action. You can only help yourself if you *realize* that your anxieties are being triggered. When you find yourself suddenly flustered, stop and take a breath. In just a few more paragraphs and all through chapter 10, you'll learn special tools curated just for *you* to use in those triggered moments.

How Lovers Flourish

Now comes the fun step. Remember, all anxiety styles have a corresponding flourish type. As humans, we often focus on the threats in our environment and the negative characteristics we believe about ourselves—and Lovers, you can be particularly hard on yourselves. So let's highlight and celebrate all the areas where you shine! Consider where the very traits that have hurt you have also served you well.

What simple actions can you take to heal, grow, and become happier and less dependent on the moods, words, and actions of others? We're going to make a list of the good stuff. What skills have you developed by being a Lover mom like Lisa? What are you particularly good at where others seem to struggle? This is the moment when your cashapona roots are soaking in loads of good, healthy sustenance. Let's embrace your flourishing Lover traits!

> **Let me ask you this, Momma:**
> Do you value and appreciate your relationships and friendships?
> Are you able to overlook others' flaws to see the good inside?
> Do you have a big and open heart?
> Can you read people really well?
> Are you transparent and honest?
> Do you notice people's moods and subtle changes in their emotional states?
> Can you communicate easily with a variety of different people?
> Are you dependable and reliable?

Do you seldom take your friends for granted?

Are you loyal and trustworthy?

Can you show and give appreciation easily?

Are you responsible and respectful of others' feelings?

Do you feel deeply when someone you care about is hurting?

Do you like these qualities about yourself? Do you value these characteristics? Do you feel proud of showing up in the world as an honest, trustworthy, responsible, and loyal friend? Wouldn't you like to have more friends who have these same qualities? Can you see that many people don't have the same skills as you? Not everyone values and prioritizes their relationships the way you do. This is where you flourish.

You are amazing, my friend! Look at that list again. From this place of gratitude and acknowledgment of your flourish type, let's focus on what you can actually do to amplify the good and shift from anxiety to embracing your power. It's important for you Lovers to know, as Gabby Bernstein says, "You are not responsible for other people's happiness. Every individual has the power to shift their own life, and you can't do it for them."

The Lover's Life Lesson

Yes, you have an intense core drive to connect with others. You feel amazing when surrounded by love and genuine attention from people you care about. However, what if your lesson in this lifetime is **to feel worthy of love *despite* the actions or words of others**? Read that again. What if your work here is to know you are worthy, no matter what. Maybe your greatest achievement is feeling deeply that you are indeed worthy of attention, worthy of affection, and worthy of love. And while this lesson might not come overnight, you can begin now with this mantra: *I am safe. I am strong. I am worthy. I belong.* Try repeating this four-part mantra every morning and night as you box-breathe: four counts inhale, four counts hold, four counts exhale, four counts hold. *I am safe* (inhale). *I am strong* (hold). *I am worthy* (exhale). *I belong* (hold). Repeat five times every morning as you wake and every night before you fall asleep. Make a slight smile on your face as you say it.

Mantras are just the first step. Incorporating the exercises in the following section is the next step. Check in with yourself. How can you show up for yourself *today*? What can you do at this moment? How can you honor and celebrate your unique skills and sensitivities and learn from them? How can you show *yourself* more attention? How can you show *yourself* more kindness? How can you show *yourself* more affection? How can you show *yourself* more love?

The Lover Self-Care Exercises and Tools

Following are specially curated strategies for you, the Lover mom. Incorporating them will allow you to reduce feelings of stress and anxiety. You can become unflustered by finding balance. I've included strategies to use once a year, once a week, once daily, and five times a day. Before you roll your eyes and ask, "Who has time for all that?" these are simple strategies you can make into habits by considering your motivational style from chapter 3. Start with just *one* of the strategies listed here—whichever one makes you smile or nod your head first. Once it's become a beneficial habit in your life, circle back to this page and start another strategy. Set a reminder, text a friend to be your accountability partner, or create a micro-goal out of it. Again, remember to use your personal motivational style to make it *easy*.

---

*Knowing what to do means little
if you don't actually do it.*

Once a Year: Have a Trigger Talk

After reading this chapter, take a moment to talk to your partner and family to share what you've learned about yourself. Refrain from blame or excuses and stick to the facts. You've realized there are certain situations or phrases that you're sensitive to. And even though you know in your heart that they're not done or said with harmful intent, they still hurt. They sting. And you feel triggered by them.

Explain calmly that when you hear your partner say, "I'm gonna be home late tonight," your brain jumps to all sorts of wild fears. It's like it skips the processing step in your logical brain (prefrontal cortex) and jumps straight to an intense emotional reaction (amygdala). Then, and this is the most important part, *give your partner words to use instead.* Tell your partner you need much more information than they might realize. For instance, they could say something like, "I'm really in the zone on this presentation, and I want it to be great for tomorrow's meeting. If I spend another hour here, I'll be so much less stressed tonight. How about we order some Thai food and have a picnic in bed when I get home?" Take responsibility and ask nicely, emphasizing that it's not them, it's *you.* Explain that it would very much help your brain to process the situation if you had a bit more detail and a plan for connecting again soon.

Remember to take full responsibility for your own emotional reactions, **ask** for their help, and give them a **specific** way to help you with potential triggering situations. Then show them genuine gratitude when they follow through. Amazingly, when your partner does this consistently, you may start to find that you need this type of detailed explanation less and less. Good luck. You can totally do this!

Once a Week: The Inner Child Meditation

You don't need years, or even weeks, of meditation experience to benefit from this practice. Before I describe the simple steps, realize that there's no "wrong" way to do this. Start by taking 10 minutes once a week to find a quiet place to sit comfortably, and begin to slow your breathing. Imagine a safe, beautiful spot in nature. It could be on a sandy beach, a crystal-blue lake high in the mountains, or a beautiful rock formation in the desert. Take a moment to imagine what you feel on your face (breeze, sunlight, raindrops), what you smell (pine, rosemary), and the sounds you hear (birds, trees ruffling in the breeze).

Once you feel as calm and serene as possible, imagine you see a small child about 20 feet away, playing quietly and happily by herself. This is *you.* The age of the child might come to you automatically. If not, start with age five. (The more trauma in your life, the younger your inner child should be.) The first week, you can just hold the child, smile at her, maybe take her by the hand and go for a walk. Send her love through your smiles and physical interaction. The second week, you might take it one step further and tell her all the things she needs to hear right now at her age. *You are worthy of love. You are perfect exactly as you are. You are worthy of attention and affection. I really, really like you. You are a super special kid.* In the third week, you can try asking your inner child what she needs or what questions she has for you.

This is all part of an emotional re-parenting of *yourself.* Only you know what you needed most as a child. With all your experiences and intimate knowledge and understanding of yourself, you are the best-equipped person to act like the parent you needed most. You can extend this further by imagining yourself at different ages. If you carry a lot of hurt and anger toward your parents, you can expand this by imagining your parents as children themselves. Can you give them the love or attention they may have lacked in their own childhoods?

Please remember to be kind to yourself. This is a healing process. Like anything, check in with your emotional bank account. If you're feeling very depleted and this process further drains you, don't do it. Hold off until you feel ready for it. This can be an incredibly healing practice. Do it with grace and understanding and self-kindness always in your heart.

Once Daily: The Nighttime Tip Jar

Find a jar, basket, or empty shoebox and put it on your nightstand. Then grab some printer paper and cut or tear it into strips, about four to six per page depending on how big you write. Every night before bed, write on a strip of paper one quality or characteristic you love and appreciate about yourself and then put it in your tip jar. Think about your superpowers: Are you considerate of others' feelings? Are you a good listener? Are you trustworthy? Are you taking the time to learn more about yourself so that you can be your best? Are you reading this awesome book so you can improve yourself and help your children? This will get easier every night, and the jar will begin to fill. Leave it open so you can see your pile growing. Feeling unlovable today? Look! You have the proof right there. Those are all the ways you are truly awesome.

Now, you're not just going to write these out, throw them in a jar, and then beat yourself up the rest of the day. Nope. When you start to bully yourself, go to the jar. Read five notes aloud. Hold one in your hand, close your eyes, and take a slow, deep breath. Is this quality important to you? Is it valuable to you? Would you like a partner or friend with this quality? Do you feel proud of yourself and grateful that you have this quality? Good. Now, hold that feeling as long as possible in your mind and in your body. This is rewiring your brain. You are purposely calling attention to your superpowers. You are healing those holes in your heart with self-love. By doing this over and over again, you are walking your roots to healthier soil, calmer weather, and more hospitable terrain.

Five Times a Day: The Worthiness Mantra

I love mantras, mostly because they are simple to do, cost-free, and can be done literally anywhere and almost any time. Oh, and they flippin' work like magic. I've used them in every area of my life for decades and continue to use them every day. Start by choosing a simple phrase. Technically, when these phrases have actual meanings, they're called *affirmations*. A *mantra* is a sound or repetition of a single word. (Use whichever term you prefer.)

The important part, my friend, is that you choose a phrase that is *challenging* for you to believe about yourself, but not ridiculously unbelievable. For instance, years ago I started a financial-related mantra. Every day, at least three or four times, I would say aloud, "I'm so grateful I have financial stability." This felt like a big leap, but not impossible. After a few years, I realized I had been financially stable for a while, so I modified the mantra to "I'm so grateful I have complete financial freedom." Now, after a few more years, I have financial freedom that I never would have thought possible when I was broke, bankrupt, and quite flustered about the price of toothpaste.

Choose a mantra that feels right for you. You can use the four-part mantra described previously or create your own. Remember, choose or create one that feels like a stretch but not a total fantasy. Focus on what you want, not what you're wanting less of. Here are some other particularly powerful sample mantras for the Lover momma:

I am so grateful I feel worthy of love.
I am so grateful I am worthy of affection.
I know my loved ones want to spend time with me.
I am worthy of love and respect.
Every day I feel more and more love and acceptance for myself.
I love and respect myself.

You may notice I begin some mantras with "I am so grateful." This is very purposeful. Beginning any journey, any shift, from a place of gratitude will amplify the message and quicken the results. Starting anything—a job, a relationship, a hobby—from a place of anger, frustration, or resentment rarely leads to a positive outcome. It works the same way with mantras. Truly feeling gratitude and saying it aloud is critical. Then attach your mantra to a habit you're already doing five times a day, like washing your hands, opening the fridge, or scrolling Instagram. It's that simple!

Let's Review

- ♥ You are more powerful when you know and notice your triggers.
- ♥ You can show self-love by articulating your needs effectively.
- ♥ You can show self-kindness by celebrating your flourish traits.
- ♥ You can show self-value when using your self-care strategies.
- ♥ You are innately worthy of love, respect, attention, and affection.

The Four-Part Breath Mantra for Lover Moms

You can go to www.ambertrueblood.com/books to download a special guided meditation and mantra practice for Lover moms.

Sit quietly. Inhale deeply. Relax your shoulders. Exhale fully. Relax your jaw. Inhale deeply. Then say the following:

> *I am safe. (inhale)*
> *I am strong. (hold)*
> *I am worthy. (exhale)*
> *I belong. (hold)*
> *(repeat)*

5

THE VISIONARY ✹

ARE YOU A VISIONARY MOM? LET'S FIND OUT. Getting to know your primary anxiety type will lead to more self-acceptance and self-kindness, less conflict with those you love, and a healthy way to navigate this life. If this is your type, this chapter will allow you to better understand yourself so you can have more of what you want in your life.

Remember Victoria? She's our Visionary mom. She feels deeply driven to make her mark in this lifetime. She has a strong desire to find her true purpose, then act on it. If you're like Victoria, you might feel frustrated watching others waste their potential. You might believe there's no point in going "small." Moms like Victoria flourish when they find clarity about what they're meant to do in this lifetime, and they feel energized when making progress toward that dream. For instance, Victoria envisions using her degree in architecture to create a network of sustainable, modern, low-cost housing for single parents. She wants to use her ambition and creativity to solve a problem that's important to her.

Anxiety flares up most when moms with this anxiety style don't know what impact they're meant to make or when something is stopping them from making progress. Whenever the daily tasks of motherhood keep Victoria from moving forward in her dream for days or weeks at a time, she feels frustrated and anxious. Visionary moms tend to be dreamers, have tremendous problem-solving skills, and persevere long after most others give up. Their priorities, values, decisions, fears, perceptions, thoughts, behaviors, and beliefs are influenced heavily by the need to feel like they're making an impact.

Victoria's unique anxiety style and flourish type might be difficult for others to understand, as they highly influence what she focuses on most. It's like a filter that translates the perceptions of the world around her. Victoria's experiences of the people she meets, the challenges she faces, and the opportunities she's offered are all filtered through this lens. When you're a Visionary, your decisions and emotions are fueled by a deep underlying desire to feel like you're achieving your life's purpose.

The Visionary Clues

As a Visionary, you might:

- Feel irritated at others who cannot appreciate the bigger picture.
- Get bored easily with mundane tasks.
- Get frustrated with rules, regulations, or the status quo.
- Find it challenging to enjoy the little moments.
- Jump from one big idea to the next, planting and starting the seed but not sticking around to tend to it long-term.
- Find that people are drawn to your energy and vision.
- Sometimes miss out on opportunities to connect with friends or family in favor of working on your big projects.
- Have very high expectations of yourself.

As a Visionary, you may notice that you don't get the same degree of satisfaction from the little joys in life as other people do. You're also less likely to let setbacks or mistakes hold you back from your intended progress. You might wonder how people with resources, connections, intellect, and opportunity don't take advantage and accomplish something big in this world. Visionary moms may love reading or hearing stories of change-makers, thought leaders, and industry disruptors. They might secretly feel confused about how other people can be satisfied living what they consider a small life.

Notice if many of these clues resonate with you. We often assume that *most* people will feel the same way we feel. If your initial response to these clues was *Well, yeah, of course, wouldn't anybody feel that way?* then this may be your anxiety type, my friend. And remember, while you may resonate most with one anxiety style or flourish type, it's likely you have a secondary type too. So keep reading.

Here's the key to really knowing if you're a Visionary: your ultimate dream would be to see your name and face gracing the cover of *Forbes* or *Vanity Fair* as the innovator of the century or the top of the "Most *Anything*" list. Maybe it feels weird to admit aloud, but secretly, would you die a happy woman if it were true? If yes, then you, my friend, are most likely a Visionary. Like all five styles, you've developed this type for good reason. It's allowed you to function with less anxiety in many areas of your life, and it's allowed you to focus on what you value most. Because you highly value striving for a big purpose in your life, with healthy habits your dreams will flourish. We need Visionaries in our world to think big, to buck the system, to achieve great things.

That's why we are not here to change who you are. No way. Instead, let's figure out the areas of this flourish type that serve you really well and celebrate those. Then we'll figure out the parts of your anxiety style that no longer serve you, and we'll learn together how to release those. Last, you'll get new communication strategies to minimize your unhealthy cycles. You deserve to go after your dreams. You're a Visionary, baby, and that is flippin' marvelous!

The Visionary Cycles

If you're still unsure about how the Visionary type applies to your life, let's touch on some common trends: You might have patterns of dreaming up big projects or businesses. Maybe you spend a lot of your time and energy daydreaming about making huge changes in an industry, building a business, or starting a foundation. Maybe you find yourself excited at the start of a big project, and listless and flustered when you don't have the time or money to actually work on it. You might become bored and irritable when most of your energy is spent on basic daily tasks. Mundane or tedious work feels mind-bogglingly awful. You might look back at your life so far and find that your happiest times were when you had a big idea and set the plan to bring it to fruition.

This anxiety style might also affect your life in more subtle ways: You may have a fear of not knowing what it is you want most to accomplish. You might feel stuck or bored often. You might find yourself distracted in groups, thinking of other things. You might feel like a dreamer, spending much of your time in your head. If you're a Visionary like our mom Victoria, you might feel expectations that no one else around you seems to feel. Friends and loved ones may try reminding you about all the wonderful parts of your life that you "should" feel gratitude for. And, when you don't feel completely satiated by your great life, you might feel guilty about it.

The Visionary's Baloney Beliefs

Understanding the "baloney beliefs" underlying your anxiety style can be challenging. While reading these might sting a bit, it's an important step in this process. By bringing these uncomfortable beliefs to the surface of your conscious mind, we can more easily dispel them—take the wind from their sails, so to speak. Baloney beliefs are the unsubstantiated, accidental beliefs you often don't even realize you hold. Let's take a moment to dredge up the baloney beliefs associated with this anxiety style. Then we can start to dismantle them together.

Remember how you're a cashapona? If your roots (beliefs) are no longer serving you, if they're no longer supporting you or feeding you nutrient-rich soil or sufficient water, let's get you moving. You can grow strong, new roots by creating healthier beliefs that support you better.

Understanding exactly how you ended up rooted in this particular spot is less important than learning the skills to move to a healthier place. The first step, though, is knowing where you are now. Where are your roots planted? What are those unsupportive beliefs that aren't serving you well? If you're a Visionary like Victoria, you may identify with many of these baloney beliefs:

- I can't slow down.
- It's a waste of my time and energy if it doesn't lead to my bigger goal.

- I can't trust others to make the right decisions.
- Life is all about the end product.
- I'm only happy when I'm moving toward my life's purpose.
- Everyone else is fine without my help.
- Nobody will remember the little things I missed.

Visionary Arianna Huffington said, "My heart is at ease knowing that what was meant for me will never miss me, and that what misses me was never meant for me."

The Visionary Contributors

You're probably thinking about where these baloney beliefs originated. How did they take hold? How did they end up coloring so much of your life? I'll touch on a few possibilities, though I invite you *not* to dwell on them. In the meantime, just know they could have been a variety of experiences—huge or tiny. There's a good chance that your baloney beliefs came from the perception that you gain your worth when you do something larger than life in this world. Somehow, your value got tangled together with not only accomplishing something but accomplishing something really big. You may have heard how your parents talked about a public figure with such admiration and respect that you subconsciously created the story that accomplishing something similar would grant you the ultimate level of love and respect from your parents. Or, maybe someone you knew directly seemed to be changing the world and you wanted to do the same.

One of the Visionary moms in my community, Kristen, watched her mom go to law school (at UC Berkeley, no less) while raising her and her two brothers. She said that after dinner each night, her mom would put the kids to bed, then leave the house and drive to the nearby grocery store. Every night, starting at 10:00 PM, her mother sat alone in her car in the lit Lucky's parking lot and studied. After law school, her mother became a juvenile probation officer for the county, which put quite a damper on Kristen's attempts at teenage debauchery and mayhem. She remembers sneaking around with a group of skater kids and trespassing onto properties with empty pools (great for skateboarding in the 1980s).

One time, the cops showed up, and snooty teenage Kristen told the officers at the scene that her mom was a probation officer. Unfortunately, this little announcement backfired. Her mother's friends at the precinct (upon her mother's urging, no doubt) gave Kristen twice the community service hours as any of her trespassing friends. Apparently, trying to be the "bad girl" wasn't going to be as easy as she'd hoped! Surely watching a smart, capable, ambitious mother of three complete law school when most women in her generation felt their options were teacher, nurse, or secretary made a deep impact on Kristen. Many moms have a big aha moment when they uncover the single childhood experience that most contributed to their anxiety style. Once they can connect the dots and better understand themselves, it's much easier to let go of any self-judgment (or shame) and move forward.

The Visionary Triggers

So now what? How do you change a lifelong anxiety style so that it no longer controls you? How do you stop any negative patterns and start new, healthier habits? Let's start with situational triggers. These are the moments when your anxiety style is being actively engaged. If you can notice a trigger while it's happening, you'll be able to more purposely *respond* instead of *react* to the situation or event.

The first step is noticing when you're being triggered. I encourage you to take a moment, right now, to identify your most common triggers. These are typical situations, people, or even phrases that leave you feeling more hurt or upset than feels appropriate for the situation. As you read the following list, circle the items that particularly spark an emotional reaction in your body.

A boss or partner gives you a pile of busy work.
Someone else announces a similar dream to yours.
A rule or regulation stands in the way of your dream.
You have a birthday and feel no closer to your dream than you were
    a year ago.
You experience a sickness, family emergency, or natural disaster that
    diverts your work.

Sometimes the same trigger will have a minor effect on you at one point but a huge impact on you at another point in time. Tolerance levels depend on your emotional fuel tank. Maybe you recently figured out exactly what your next big step is. At this point, you're feeling energized and focused. If your partner asked you to take out the trash and help the kids with their homework, you might happily oblige. (Your emotional reserve tank is nice and full.) However, if you received an e-mail from the city planning office denying your permits, and then your partner asked you for help with the trash and kids' homework, you might lose your shit. (Your tank is low.) Kristen says that when she found out another company in her area of expertise was advertising the same sort of offer, she felt extremely frustrated and considered stopping her program entirely. Like many Visionary moms, she finds the technical details of her business highly distracting and energy draining. Kristen works best when the path is cleared ahead so that she can do what she loves, learn from others, and be the creative visionary in her business.

Understanding and acknowledging your triggers is an important key to insight and taking action. You can only help yourself if you *realize* that your anxieties are being triggered. When you find yourself suddenly flustered, stop and take a breath. In just a few more paragraphs and all through chapter 10, you'll learn special tools curated just for *you* to use in those triggered moments.

How Visionaries Flourish

Now comes the fun step. Remember, all anxiety styles have associated flourish types. As humans, we often focus on the threats in our environment and the negative characteristics we believe about ourselves, and Visionaries can have particularly high expectations of themselves. So let's highlight and celebrate all the areas where you shine! Consider where the very traits that have hurt you have also served you well.

What simple actions can you take to heal, grow, and become happier and less dependent on whether or not you've accomplished your ultimate purpose in this life? We're going to make a list of the good stuff. What skills have you developed by being a Visionary mom like Victoria? What are you particularly good at, where others seem to struggle? This is the moment when your cashapona roots are soaking in loads of good, healthy sustenance. Let's embrace your Visionary superpowers!

Let me ask you this, Momma:
Can see solutions to problems that few others can see?
Do you feel passionate about a cause bigger than yourself?
Do you truly value the dedicated and honest people around you?
Do you see the bigger picture more easily than most?
Do you feel confident talking to a variety of people?
Can you articulate your dreams with enthusiasm and excitement?
Do you avoid getting distracted by little setbacks that might stop others?
Are you honorable, focused, and passionate when you set your mind on a goal?

Do you like these qualities about yourself? Do you value these characteristics? Do you feel proud of showing up in the world as a focused, driven, passionate dreamer? Wouldn't you like to have more friends with these same qualities? Do you agree that many people don't have these superpowers?

You are incredible, my friend! Look at that list again. From this place of gratitude and acknowledgment of your special skills, let's focus on what you can actually do to amplify the good of your flourish type and minimize any negative aspects of your anxiety.

The Visionary's Life Lesson

What if your lesson in this life is **to enjoy the little things on your way to achieving your life's purpose**? What if you could slow down and still feel energized and excited? What if you could connect more deeply with those you love? What if you could be more present in the moment with your family? What if you could listen more to those you love and respect? What if you could get the same amount of satisfaction from the little things in life as the big things? What if you could slow down enough to enjoy the journey you're on as you achieve your big life's purpose?

The Visionary Self-Care Exercises and Tools

Here are the handpicked strategies for you, the Visionary mom. Incorporating these tools will allow you to reduce feelings of stress and anxiety because they specifically balance out those areas where your anxiety style isn't supporting your needs. I've included strategies to use once a year, once a week, once daily, and five times a day. Before you roll your eyes and ask, "Who has time for all that?" these are simple strategies that you can make into habits by considering your motivational style from chapter 3. Start with just one of the strategies listed below—whichever one makes you smile or nod your head first. Once it's become a beneficial habit in your life, circle back to this page and start another strategy. Set a reminder, text a friend to be your accountability partner, or create a micro-goal out of it. Again, remember to use your personal motivational style to make it *easy*.

> *Knowing what to do means little*
> *if you don't actually do it.*

Once a Year: Tiny Moments

Once a year, take 30 minutes to jot down the highlights of the previous year. Try to focus not only on the big accomplishments, but also on the *moments* you enjoyed. Think about the people you care about most in your life. What were some of the experiences or memories you remember fondly from the previous year? Think about your physical senses. Can you recall the most beautiful scene or sunset you witnessed? Can you remember a song you loved hearing? Can you think of a particular dish you enjoyed because of its flavor or the company you enjoyed while you ate it?

As a Visionary, it's often easy to forget how much joy you got from the tiny moments in your life. Taking 30 minutes just once a year to purposefully recall those tiny moments will make it more likely you'll enjoy even more of those moments this coming year. You may find you're better able to cherish the very moments that might have seemed an irritable distraction before now. By writing down the tiny moments you enjoyed, you may feel less flustered the next time you hit speed bumps on your path to achieving your life's purpose.

Once a Week: The Reconnect

The weekly practice for Visionary moms is to regularly and purposefully connect with the people you love. Acknowledging your loved ones by the time you spend with them and the attention you give to them is a fantastic way to strengthen your emotional connections. Take the time to listen attentively to what's on their mind, then validate their feelings and emotions. In this practice, you'll want to carve time out of your schedule and out of your to-do list to connect with someone you care about. Let the conversation be primarily about them. Ask open-ended questions. Empathize with them genuinely. Make eye contact. And don't give them suggestions or advice unless they *specifically* ask for it. Reconnecting with those you care about on a weekly basis will not only deepen your relationships, it will also serve to encourage those people to stick by you and support you on your journey toward achieving your life's purpose. In the end, if you're sitting in a hospital bed with your *Forbes* issue proudly displayed on your bedside table, it'll be even more satisfying if you're also surrounded by those who happily cheered you on the entire way.

*"Success is nothing without someone
you love to share it with."*
—Billy Dee Williams

Once Daily: You're Grounded!

Visionary moms spend much of their time with their head in the clouds and their mind spinning with ideas and plans. Taking five minutes a day to ground yourself, literally, can help you both physically and emotionally. Grounding can look like walking outside in bare feet on the grass, dirt, or sand. It can also look like taking a bath, jumping in a pool, or even taking a hot shower. As Sylvia Plath said, "There must be quite a few things that a hot bath won't cure, but I don't know many of them."

Do a five-minute grounding activity each day, preferably right before bed. Leave your phone in another room if you're in the bath. Leave your phone inside the house if you're outside. Just really take it all in. If you're outside, breathe the fresh air in deeply. Look up at the sky and watch the trees. Listen and take note of the most subtle sound you hear. What can you smell? Breathe. If you're in a bath or shower, watch the water dripping down the tile wall. Close your eyes and listen to the sounds of the water as you move around. What can you smell? Breathe deeply and slowly.

You may find that the first time you do this, even more ideas and brilliant strategies pop urgently into your head. You might also find that solutions to long-held problems become immediately visible. It's OK. That's normal. When you come back inside or when you get out of the bath, you can write them all down. Eventually, as you practice this more often, your mind slows and the solutions and intuitive impulses come even without taking the time to ground yourself. Also, you'll find you can hold onto the ideas longer in your mind. You don't have to immediately jot them down. They arrive in a calm mind, so they're not as elusive as they once were. For Visionaries, a nightly grounding practice can not only help you feel less flustered and improve your sleep, it can also speed up your journey toward achieving your life's purpose.

Five Times a Day: Tiny Pleasures Practice

Find a box, basket, or big jar and place it next to your refrigerator. Then grab some notebook paper or printer paper (or, if you wanna get fancy, find nice colored stationery paper) and cut it into four-by-four inch squares. Every time you make a meal or grab a glass of water (or wine), jot down a tiny thing you're grateful for. Eventually, you can just say it aloud every time you see the jar (or every time you open the refrigerator). For instance, "I'm so grateful that the reimbursement check came in the mail today!" Or, "I'm so grateful I got to see my friend Dana today!" Or, "I'm so grateful my podcast interview on *Honest as a Mother* went so well today!" Or, "I'm so grateful I didn't have to cook dinner tonight and got to work on my book instead!" Or, "I'm so grateful I found out I got booked again on *Good Day LA* for next week!" (Yes, those are my personal tiny pleasures for today.) When Visionary moms consciously take time throughout their day to focus on the tiny pleasures in their lives, they're far less likely to feel anxious, flustered, and frustrated.

Let's Review

- You are more powerful when you know and notice your triggers.
- You can show self-love by articulating your needs effectively.
- You can show self-kindness by celebrating your skills and talents.
- You can show self-value when using your self-care strategies.
- You are innately worthy of love, respect, attention, and affection.

The Four-Part Breath Mantra for Visionary Moms

You can go to www.ambertrueblood.com/books to download a special guided meditation and mantra practice for Visionary Moms.

Sit quietly. Inhale deeply. Relax your shoulders. Exhale fully. Relax your jaw. Inhale deeply. Then say the following:

> *I tune in. (exhale)*
> *I am here. (hold)*
> *I hold the light. (inhale)*
> *My path is clear. (hold)*
> *(repeat)*

6

THE DYNAMO ★

ARE YOU A DYNAMO MOM? LET'S FIND OUT. Getting to know your primary anxiety style and corresponding flourish type will lead to more self-acceptance and self-kindness, less conflict with those you love, and a healthy way to navigate life. If this is your type, this chapter will allow you to better understand yourself so you can have more of what you want in your life.

Remember Daisy? She's the Dynamo mom who truly thrives when she feels valued by others. One of her deepest motivators is earning respect and acknowledgment through her achievements. If you're like Daisy, you also thrive when accomplishing tasks and goals, planning, organizing, and checking items off your to-do list. Daisy's anxiety flares up most when she feels like she's not meeting her own high expectations for herself. Unlike many moms, she feels flustered when she's not going a million miles per hour.

Contributors to developing this anxiety style vary greatly from person to person. Often, people like Daisy have a parent they love and respect who is also a Dynamo. They might have been a high achiever in school, receiving accolades and attention that felt really good. Women with this style of anxiety might also have experienced teasing or bullying in school, leaving them questioning their intrinsic worthiness. Whatever the cause, women like Daisy tend to focus on achievement in an attempt to garner the respect and acknowledgment they so deeply crave. As a result, their priorities, values, decisions, fears, perceptions, thoughts, behaviors, and beliefs are influenced heavily by the need to feel valued and appreciated by others. For instance, Daisy loves big projects like leading the new initiative her company created to reach and support B-corporations that are driven not only by profit but also by their mission. Like her buddy Victoria, she's energized by accomplishing and creating new projects such as the B-corp finance initiative. Unlike Victoria, Daisy has the attention to detail and the daily drive to do even the mundane tasks, as long as her loved ones or peers acknowledge and appreciate her effort.

Your anxiety style cultivates a combination of traits and abilities to bring you more of what is most important to you by making you anxious about traits that may threaten your ability to reach that goal. In the case of the Dynamo, the goal or need is feeling respected and acknowledged for your accomplishments. Daisy's unique anxiety style might be difficult for others to understand, as it highly influences what she focuses on most. It's like a filter that translates the perceptions of the world around her. Daisy's experiences of the people she meets, the challenges she faces, and the opportunities she's offered are all filtered through this lens. When you're a Dynamo, your decisions and emotions are fueled by a deep underlying desire to feel respected and valued by others.

The Dynamo Clues

If this is your anxiety style, you're likely to feel flustered or resentful when:

- ★ Your achievements go unnoticed or uncelebrated.
- ★ You feel condescended to by others.
- ★ People in your field become successful or receive accolades.
- ★ You feel like you're not living up to your own high standards.
- ★ You feel disrespected or aren't taken seriously.
- ★ Someone says "don't worry about it" or "shushes" you.
- ★ You don't have any challenging projects to work on.
- ★ You feel like you're stagnating or living in a "Groundhog Day" world.
- ★ You feel like you've failed.

If you're a Dynamo, you may find yourself starting new jobs, switching careers, or signing up for certification programs and courses more often than the other women in your life. You might say yes to projects or responsibilities you don't necessarily want to do or even enjoy. Dynamo women often feel an adrenaline high when completing tasks or solving complex problems. At the end of a particularly challenging day, these women often feel energized and fulfilled rather than emotionally drained. Emergencies are met with decisive action. These moms tend to enjoy big, hard challenges and feel little satisfaction completing routine or mundane tasks. Dynamo women often thrive in an environment of change and constantly look to their next goal—often without celebrating or acknowledging their most recent accomplishment.

If you're a Dynamo, you might find yourself creating tasks or projects to do just so you can feel a sense of accomplishment when they're complete. You might feel frustrated or depressed at the end of a day in which you didn't accomplish "enough." You might get angry or upset if someone gets (or takes) credit for your idea or hard work. You might find yourself sad or hurt if a loved one doesn't acknowledge your accomplishments. You might also get easily frustrated with people who cannot work as efficiently and effectively as you can.

Notice if many of these clues resonate with you. We often assume that *most* people would feel the same way we feel. If your initial response to these clues was, *Well, yeah, of course, wouldn't anybody feel that way?* then this may be your anxiety style, my friend. (Remember what you learned in part I: while you may resonate with one anxiety style most, we all identify with a few types to varying degrees.)

Here's the key to really knowing if you're a Dynamo: When you solve a big problem or accomplish a big project, do you feel that adrenaline high? Are you energized and excited? When someone seeks you out to acknowledge your efforts, do you feel a surge of joy and pride? When you set out to accomplish a big, audacious goal, do you feel more excited than hesitant? Like all five anxiety styles and flourish types, you've developed this set of traits for good reason. They've allowed you to function with less anxiety in many areas of your life, and allowed you to focus on what you value most.

Listen, we are not here to change who you are. No way. Instead, let's figure out the areas of this flourish type that serve you really well and celebrate those. Then we'll figure out the parts of your anxiety style that no longer serve you, and we'll learn together how to release those. Last, you'll get new communication strategies to minimize your unhealthy cycles. You deserve acknowledgment and respect. You're a Dynamo baby, and that is flippin' fierce!

The Dynamo Cycles

If you're still unsure about how this flourish type applies to your life, let's touch on some common trends.

Dynamos tend to:

★   Begin lots of big projects, jobs, or degrees or take on big respon-sibilities in their families (over and over again).

★   Function with a workload that is just on the edge of too much, so that when something unforeseen happens, it often teeters over that edge.

★   Find themselves consistently planning or daydreaming about the future, seldom tuning in and enjoying the present.

★   Have difficulty with inaction (meditation, waiting in lines, talk-ing to people who speak . . . very . . . slow . . . ly).

★   Admire other high achievers, but feel drawn to in-the-moment people who naturally slow down and easily enjoy the present moment.

This anxiety style might also affect your life in more subtle ways. Anxiety about accomplishing the next big thing might keep you from enjoying the last big thing you accomplished. It might also put you down a path you consider more respectable or admirable even if the path you truly want to travel is different. You might find that you lose friend-ships or relationships because you perceive a lack of drive or internal motivation as a frustrating character flaw. You might struggle with find-ing a balance between slowing down to be in the present moment and still doing the work you love at the pace you enjoy. At this point, you might benefit from shifting your self-worth to internal measures instead of relying on reactions or accolades from others. As media mogul and author Arianna Huffington wrote, "Life is a dance between making it happen and letting it happen."

The Dynamo's Baloney Beliefs

Understanding the "baloney beliefs" underlying your anxiety style can be challenging. While reading these might sting a bit, it's an important step in this process. By bringing these uncomfortable beliefs to the surface of your conscious mind, we can dispel them more easily—take the wind from their sails, so to speak. Baloney beliefs are the unsubstantiated, accidental beliefs you often don't even realize you hold. If you're a Dynamo, let's take a moment to dredge up the beliefs most often associated with this anxiety style. That way, we can start to dismantle them together.

Remember how you're a cashapona? If your roots (beliefs) are no longer serving you, if they're no longer supporting you or feeding you nutrient-rich soil or sufficient water, let's get you moving. You can grow strong, new roots by creating healthier beliefs that support you better.

Understanding exactly how you ended up rooted in this particular spot is less important than learning the skills to move to a healthier place. The first step, though, is knowing where you are now. Where are your roots planted? What are those unsupportive beliefs that aren't serving you well? If you're a Dynamo like Daisy, you may identify with many of these beliefs:

* I am unworthy of love just being me.
* I am not worthy of acknowledgment unless I do something to earn it.
* I have to achieve big things to earn love, affection, or attention from others.
* I cannot be still.
* People are lazy and flaky.
* I am not doing enough.
* I cannot start until I know the entire plan will work.

★ I haven't accomplished enough today/this year/in this lifetime.
★ I have to accomplish in order to be respected.

The Dynamo Contributors

You're probably thinking about where these beliefs originated. How did they take hold? How did they end up coloring so much of your life? I'll touch on a few possibilities, though I invite you *not* to dwell on them. In the meantime, just know they could have been a variety of experiences—huge or tiny. There's a good chance that your baloney beliefs came from modeling after one of your childhood caregivers. Even very subtle reactions or situations from childhood could easily set you up for a lifetime of seeking accomplishment in hopes of feeling attention and love from others. For instance, your guide here is a Dynamo (yeah, me). When I finished writing my first book, my father jokingly responded with, "Well, now you're going to go to law school, right?" In my household, there wasn't a lot of celebration. I internalized those law school–type comments and the lack of accolades as believing maybe I hadn't done enough. I hadn't gone big enough. I hadn't accomplished it quickly enough. For me, still to this day, sooner is better. When my publishing editor asked what publication date I'd like for this book, I almost didn't understand the question. *As soon as possible, of course!* Now, I consciously ask myself, *Does this really need to be done right now?*

Somewhere along the line in early development, moms with this style "learned" their value is based heavily on accomplishment after accomplishment. Many moms have a big aha moment when they uncover the single childhood experience that most contributed to their anxiety style. Once they can connect the dots and better understand themselves, it's much easier to let go of the self-judgment (or shame) and move forward. The tricky part is that we Dynamo moms really like accomplishing, so there's an internal motivation mixed up with an external motivation. The key is getting clear and honest with yourself about what you're doing for *yourself*, because you really want to do it, and what you're doing just for validation from others.

The Dynamo Triggers

So now what? How do you change a lifelong anxiety style so that it no longer controls you? How do you stop those negative patterns and start new, healthier habits? Let's start with situational triggers. These are the moments when your anxiety style is being actively engaged. If you can notice a trigger while it's happening, you'll be able to more purposely *respond* instead of *react* to the situation or event.

The first step is noticing when you've been triggered. I encourage you to take a moment, right now, to identify your most common triggers. These are typical situations or phrases that leave you feeling more hurt or upset than feels "appropriate" for the situation. As you read the following list, circle the items that spark a tender spot for you.

Criticism or negative feedback on your work
Losing a job or not getting a promotion
Earning less than you made the previous year
Experiencing an external challenge that prevents you from working toward a goal (weather, physical injury, long illness, etc.)
Having to work or interact with people who don't share your work ethic
Perceived failure
Long periods of time doing mundane or repetitive tasks

Author Kate Northrup, a fellow Dynamo, writes, "What I've found is that when I focus on managing my energy instead of managing my time, I end up having enough time for the things that really matter to me." (Her book and planner, *Do Less*, is the perfect book for Dynamo moms.)

Sometimes the same trigger will have a minor effect on you at one point but a huge impact on you at another point in time. Tolerance levels depend on your emotional fuel tank. Maybe you recently received an award and attended a beautiful ceremony and reception. At this point, you're feeling respected and acknowledged for all your efforts. If you get criticism about your proposal from your boss, you're more likely to handle it well emotionally. (Your tank is nice and full.) However, if you accidentally missed an important deadline, had a day where you felt as if you accomplished nothing, then opened the e-mail from your boss about your poorly written proposal, you might feel extremely flustered and upset. (Your tank is low, my friend.)

I get triggered most on days when I feel like all my time and energy was spent doing never-ending tasks. No matter how much laundry I do, there will be three more loads tomorrow. Every morning I sweep the kitchen floor, but it's gross by the end of the day. No matter when I make meals, everyone still wants to eat three hours later. (What the heck, right?) Now I use the "add a joy" practice from the end of this chapter. For instance, right now my bathrooms are really dirty, the laundry mountain on my sofa has reached epic proportions, and the boys have made a tower of empty laundry baskets into a fort for our cat, Andi. Instead of dealing with any of that, I am sitting across the street in my neighbor's backyard, using her quiet deck and Wi-Fi to write this chapter. By spending at least some of my time and energy every day on work that's important to me, my anxiety and frustration almost completely disappear. The high I get from writing 3,000 words keeps me going strong through the mountain of mundane, never-ending mom tasks.

Understanding and acknowledging your triggers is an important key to insight and taking action. You can only help yourself when you *realize* that your anxieties are being triggered. When you find yourself suddenly flustered, stop and take a breath. In just a few more paragraphs and all through chapter 10, you'll learn special tools curated just for *you* to use in these triggered moments.

How Dynamos Flourish

Now comes the fun step. Remember, all anxiety styles have corresponding flourish types. As humans, we often focus on the threats in our environment and the negative characteristics we believe about ourselves, and Dynamos can have particularly high expectations for themselves. So let's highlight and celebrate all the areas where you shine! Consider where the very traits that have hurt you have also served you well.

> **Let me ask you this, Momma:**
> Are you more self-motivated than most?
> Do you have really good communication skills?

Do you accomplish more in an hour than most people accomplish in a day (or even a week)?

Are you energized by challenges that others view as daunting?

Do you happily drop everything to help someone or solve a big problem?

Do you often find smarter ways to accomplish things?

Are you really good at planning and organizing?

Do friends, family members, and coworkers come to you when they need help with a big problem or event?

Do you like these qualities about yourself? Do you value these characteristics? Do you feel proud of showing up in the world as a dependable, productive, responsible, self-motivated person? Wouldn't you like to have more friends and colleagues who have these same qualities? Do you agree that many people don't have these skills?

You are amazing, my friend! Look at that list again. From this place of gratitude and acknowledgment of your special skills, let's focus on what you can actually do to amplify the good and minimize the negative aspects of this flourish type.

The Dynamo's Life Lesson

What if your lesson in this life is **to feel valuable, regardless of your accomplishments or accolades**? As Eleanor Roosevelt said, "You wouldn't worry so much about what others think of you if you realized how seldom they do." Maybe your biggest challenge as a Dynamo mom is knowing you are indeed worthy of love and acknowledgment just as you are. And while this lesson may not come overnight, you can begin now with this mantra: *I am enough. I can slow down. I am in this moment.* The first step is acknowledging what you might be missing out on by constantly striving and pushing forward. What would happen if you slowed down a bit? How might you be able to show up differently for yourself, for your partner, or for your children? How could you still feel the exhilaration of accomplishment without waiting to see what others think or feel about it? What if you could enjoy the vacation you're on now instead of already planning the next one in your mind? How can you become more present, get your value from within, and still hold all of your drive that makes you a Dynamo?

The Dynamo Self-Care Exercises and Tools

Here are the handpicked strategies for you, the Dynamo mom. Incorporating these tools will allow you to reduce feelings of stress and anxiety because they specifically balance out those areas where your anxiety style isn't supporting your needs. I've included strategies to use once a year, once a week, once daily, and five times a day. Before you roll your eyes and ask, "Who has time for all that?" these are simple strategies that you can make into habits by considering your motivational style from chapter 3. Start with just one of these strategies listed here—whichever one makes you smile or nod your head first. Once that strategy becomes a beneficial habit in your life, circle back to this page and start another strategy. Set a reminder, text a friend to be your accountability partner, or create a micro-goal out of it. Again, remember to use your personal motivational style to make it *easy*.

> *Knowing what to do means little if you don't actually do it.*

Once a Year: Add a Joy-Only Practice

Often, as adults, and especially as moms, we stop doing the things we love if they don't contribute to the finances, safety, future, or health of our families. Maybe you loved to knit or dance or play the piano. But, once your life became focused on your children and work and relationships, you were lucky to floss your teeth once a week. There are other benefits, deep benefits, to doing something every week that brings you happiness. You'll find that doing something you love, just for the mere joy of it, has an emotional ripple effect. Adding that one joyful activity magically lessens the weight of the responsibilities you carry every day. Doing something that releases dopamine and endorphins in your brain will lift your mood and increase your capacity for patience and compassion.

This is a particularly good strategy for Dynamos since they're so good at challenging themselves, setting goals, and self-motivating. However, instead of using those skills for achievement purposes, we're going to align them with activities that bring you joy. If you need to quantify this so it feels more concrete, you can count the number of minutes you spend in joy per week. An added benefit is that learning something new often requires all of your focus. Therefore, you'll be forced to focus on the present moment instead of jumping ahead in your mind to plan or prepare for the next big thing.

Even if you're super sleep deprived from caring for a newborn or an elderly parent, I have a recommendation for how you can realistically do this. I call it "the sourdough starter." Let me explain: When bakers make a new batch of sourdough bread, they set aside a small mixture of flour and water (and *lactobacilli* and yeast) to start their next loaves later. These starters are "fed" and nurtured for years, decades, and beyond. I'm no baker, but I *love* the idea of keeping a small part of *yourself* alive and "fed" during those months when virtually all your time and energy is spent feeding the needs of others.

Create a "starter" for *yourself*. Maybe it's a hobby you keep up with once a week, a journal you write in, or a new skill you take time learning in tiny bits and pieces. Feed and nurture your starter throughout these years of semi-selfless exhaustion. Then, once you have more time and energy to spend on your own needs and wants, you'll have a place to begin. You won't have to start from scratch to figure out who you are and what you enjoy. Whether you're a new mom or a seasoned parent ready to compete at the Olympic level, you can benefit from adding a joy-only practice into your life on a regular basis. Maybe you've always wanted to learn French, take salsa lessons, or play the guitar. Often, our joy-only practice is something we did for many years yet gave up because, well, "life happened."

Did you know that Vera Wang began her fashion career at the age of 40? Or that Julia Child released her first cookbook at the age of 50? Remember watching *Little House on the Prairie* on your boulder-sized living room TV while sitting on shag carpeting? Well, Laura Ingalls Wilder was 65 when she published her first book, *Little House in the*

Big Woods. And have you ever heard of Gladys Burrill? She's the badass who ran her first marathon at age 86. Now, I'm not saying you have to start a multimillion-dollar company or run marathons in your 80s. You can do almost anything you want—besides maybe helicopter skiing or BASE jumping. Those activities sound expensive and dangerous, and I'm not sure my insurance would cover you if something happened and you blamed this book. Other than that, I think you're good.

Once a Week: Open Creative Time

Dynamos can benefit from creative activities where no end goal is involved. Creative pursuits are good for women with this anxiety style because there are no right answers or wrong answers. It's time for the mind and body to act without attempting to achieve anything in particular. Writing, dancing, drawing, or singing are great places to start. These sorts of activities will help reduce your fluster, refill your emotional fuel tank, and allow your mind to slow down a bit. Even activities like ping-pong or doing puzzles could work, unless you find yourself becoming competitive and keeping score obsessively. When I began meditating, for instance, I learned that you should try to slow down your breathing rate. Immediately, that became the game for me, the challenge: 10-second exhale, then 15, then 20. Yes! I was winning! (Not sure what award I imagined receiving for that, but as a Dynamo, my achievement-oriented focus was tough to break.)

Then I attended a biohacking meditation retreat and mentioned this practice to the Harvard PhD leading our workshop. (I undoubtedly hoped he'd be super impressed by my incredibly slow breath rate.) Instead he said, "Hmm. Try focusing on the feeling of your hands touching your legs, not the breathing." Dang! He totally ruined the game for me. I begrudgingly understood his point, though. Meditation and mindfulness are about allowing yourself to just be, to notice, to accept what is without judgment or opinion or pushing yourself. I was doing it all wrong! I learned from meditation teacher Emily Fletcher that the only way you can do meditation "wrong" is to realize when you're distracted by a thought, and then consciously choose to keep thinking it instead of letting it go.

Once Daily: Shower Mindfulness Practice

In addition to the open creative practice, Dynamos can benefit immensely from a daily mindfulness practice. I highly recommend—especially if you're working remotely or are a stay-at-home-mom—taking a mindfulness shower in the mid to late afternoon. In the shower, it's unlikely (I hope) that you'll have your phone or any other devices to distract you. It's also unlikely that you'll be disturbed (lock the door if possible) or suddenly decide to unload the dishwasher. And please don't start cleaning the shower while you're in there. Instead, take a few minutes to tune in to your senses. Watch the water dripping down the tile wall. Close your eyes and notice the smell of the soap. Listen to the subtle changes in the sound of the falling water as you move around in the spray. Taste the chardonnay notes on your tongue. Oh, did I not mention I also sometimes bring in a small cup of wine? (Please don't do this if you have the proclivity to drink irresponsibly.)

You can also add a mantra practice to your mindfulness shower. For instance, if you find your mind spinning in circles, either replaying scenes from the day or planning out the next part of your evening, try repeating an affirmation: *I am so grateful my loved ones are safe, happy, healthy, and together.* The mindfulness shower can allow you to reset your nervous system and essentially refill your emotional cup so that you can feel calmer and more centered for the remainder of your day. I recommend taking this shower anytime between 3:00 and 6:00 PM, since that's typically the time when most of the humans in your home are hungry, flustered, tense, and tired and have little patience or compassion left to give. Modeling self-care like this to your children is a fantastic way for them to learn from your example. Maybe they too need a reset shower or an outside break in nature to refill their emotional cup for the evening. As Anne Lamott, one of my favorite authors, says, "Almost everything will work again if you unplug it for a few minutes, including you."

Five Times a Day: An Affirmation Practice

I'm a big fan of affirmations and mantras. I read Napoleon Hill's *Think and Grow Rich* in my early 20s, and that old book birthed many of the self-development concepts and practices popular today. Affirmations are one of those fabulous tools. Maintaining focus is virtually impossible in this world of constant distractions and pulls for our attention. I love affirmations because they serve as a reminder of what we value most at this point in our lives. They help keep us pointing in the right direction. I recommend using mantras or affirmations four to five times each day as a reminder and inspiration to realign and refocus your time and energy.

Affirmations work best when kept consistent for at least a few weeks, so you'll want to choose one that:

你 can remember easily,
highlights what is truly important to you, and
feels like a reach goal (but not an impossible goal).

For instance, "Every day I am learning to be kinder to myself."

This practice is great for Dynamos because it's so easy for them to get swept away by the thrill of achievement and the busyness of life. If you don't already have a mantra or an affirmation practice, I recommend linking your mantra to something you already do four to five times a day—for instance, using the restroom, checking your e-mail, getting stuck at a red light, or seeing an annoying post on Instagram. For Dynamo moms, I love the affirmation, "I am in this moment." You can repeat it and switch up the emphasis each time. For instance, say it five times consecutively, "*I* am in this moment. I *am* in this moment. I am *in* this moment. I am in *this* moment. I am in this *moment.*"

Let's Review

★ You are more powerful when you know and notice your triggers.

★ You can show self-love by articulating your needs effectively.

★ You can show self-kindness by celebrating your skills and talents.

★ You can show self-value when using your self-care strategies.

★ You are innately worthy of love, respect, attention, and affection.

The Four-Part Breath Mantra for Dynamo Moms

You can go to www.ambertrueblood.com/books to download a special guided meditation and mantra practice for Dynamo moms.

Sit quietly. Inhale deeply. Relax your shoulders. Exhale fully. Relax your jaw. Inhale deeply. Then say the following:

> *I slow down. (exhale)*
> *I tune in. (hold)*
> *Knowing happiness (inhale)*
> *lies within. (hold)*
> *(repeat)*

7

THE EXECUTIVE ■

ARE YOU AN EXECUTIVE MOM? LET'S FIND OUT. Getting to know your primary anxiety style flourish type will lead to more self-acceptance and self-kindness, less conflict with those you love, and a healthy way to navigate this life. If this is your type, this chapter will allow you to better understand yourself so you can have more of what you want in your life.

Remember Elizabeth? She's the Executive mom who truly values stability and structure. She learned over the years that she feels calmer and more confident when she knows what lies ahead. Even if it's difficult or a challenge, as long as Elizabeth knows about it, she can minimize her stress and anxiety levels through her genius preparation skills. It's the unknown and unforeseeable events that often throw Executive moms off their game.

Contributing factors to this style might vary greatly, but they share a common underlying thread. You might be like Elizabeth, who grew up in a military family, moving every few years to a new area or even a new country. Or you could have had parents who split up early in your life and spent time in multiple homes, with multiple parental figures, celebrating holidays in different places from year to year. You could have had parents who stayed married and in the same home for your entire childhood, but one parent had mental health issues or alcoholism. Virtually any situation resulting a home life that felt unstable, uncertain, or unsafe could lead to a person developing the Executive anxiety style. And just like siblings who grow up with the same genetics and in the same environment don't have the same priorities or personalities, siblings may also have different anxiety styles. Individuals perceive the same situations differently. A parental divorce might affect one child deeply, while their twin might go relatively unscathed.

If you're like Elizabeth, you thrive when you feel safe and secure emotionally. So you prioritize keeping things in order and planning ahead whenever possible. The more sense of control you have over a situation, the more likely you will feel happy and content. Alternatively, when you feel uncertain and unprepared for the future, your heart starts to race and your anxiety alarms begin to blare. Elizabeth developed this anxiety style because early in her life she felt the best way to reduce her fluster and overwhelm was to feel safe and secure in her daily life. So that's where she directs most of her attention. As a result, Elizabeth's priorities, values, decisions, fears, perceptions, thoughts, behaviors, and beliefs are influenced heavily by the need to feel secure and in control of her environment.

As an Executive mom, you develop this anxiety style to focus on what is most important to you—feeling *emotionally* safe. Elizabeth's unique anxiety style might be difficult for others to understand, because it highly influences what she attends to most. It's like a filter that translates the perceptions of the world around her. Elizabeth's experience of the people she meets, the challenges she faces, and the opportunities she's offered are all translated through this lens. When you're an Executive, your decisions and emotions are fueled by a deep underlying desire to feel emotionally secure in an uncertain world.

The Executive Clues

If this is your anxiety style, you're likely to feel flustered or upset when you cannot anticipate what might happen in the future. If friends, family, or your employer changes their plans or expectations of you, it can feel unsettling and stressful. You may seek to calm your anxieties by planning and scheduling your life to the nth degree. Sometimes, you might even feel embarrassed because you're not comfortable being flexible in the moment. People who live spontaneously can seem both admirable and disconcerting.

Notice if many of these clues resonate with you. We often assume that *most* people would feel the same way we feel. If your initial response to these clues was *Well, yeah, of course, wouldn't anybody feel that way?* then this may be your anxiety style, my friend. (Remember what you learned in part I: while you may resonate with one type most, we all identify with a few styles to varying degrees.) Here's a key to really know if you're an Executive mom: while you might be attracted to those who can live carefree and spontaneously, their actions can drive you crazy and cause a lot of anxiety. Like all five anxiety styles, you've developed this style for good reason. It's allowed you to function with less anxiety in many areas of your life, and it's allowed you to focus on what you value most. Because you highly value feeling safe and in control in your life, with healthy habits your relationships flourish. As an Executive mom, it's likely your friends and relatives admire and lean on your skills of organization, management, and sense of responsibility. You might be the one everyone looks to when planning a family vacation or a holiday get-together or a big work event. These flourish traits are the skills and talents you've acquired over the years, and you might not even realize how much other people value and appreciate them.

That's why we are not here to change who you are. No way. Instead, let's figure out the areas of this flourish type that serve you really well and celebrate those. Then we'll figure out the parts of your anxiety style that no longer serve you, and we'll learn together how to release those. Last, you'll get new communication strategies to minimize your unhealthy cycles. You deserve appreciation and happiness. You're an Executive, baby, and that is flippin' fantastic!

The Executive Cycles

If you're still unsure about how being an Executive mom applies to your life, let's touch on some common trends. You may tend to watch the news more than you want to so you know what might or might not be coming your way. You may have a tricky relationship with money, wanting to spend freely on food, shelter, gas, and insurance policies, but feel uncomfortable or even irresponsible spending money on luxury experiences or traveling. You may have difficulty falling asleep at night, imagining all the possible disasters or tragedies that could befall you or your family.

This anxiety style might also affect your life in more subtle ways. You may fear moving to a new city, changing your kids' schools, or losing your job. Even positive change can be stressful and anxiety-provoking. Getting a promotion, moving to a nicer home, or starting a new relationship can feel scary and unsettling. Sometimes, Executive moms feel guilty when they cannot seem to embrace and enjoy change like those around them. This need for structure and certainty can feel isolating and exhausting as well. It takes a lot of emotional energy to be this vigilant. Letting someone else take the reins once in a while is a worthy goal. Let's remember what Helen Keller said: "Security is mostly a superstition. Life is either a daring adventure or nothing."

The Executive's Baloney Beliefs

Understanding the "baloney beliefs" underlying your anxiety style can be challenging. While reading these might sting a bit, it's an important step in this process. By bringing these uncomfortable beliefs to the surface of your conscious mind, we can more easily dispel them. Take the wind from their sails, so to speak. Baloney beliefs are the unsubstantiated, accidental beliefs you often don't even realize you hold. If you're an Executive, let's take a moment to dredge up the baloney beliefs associated with this anxiety style. That way, we can start to dismantle them together.

Remember how you're a cashapona? If your roots (beliefs) are no longer serving you, if they're no longer supporting you or feeding you nutrient-rich soil or sufficient water, let's get you moving. You can grow strong, new roots by creating healthier beliefs that support you better.

Understanding exactly how you ended up rooted in this particular spot is less important than learning the skills to move to a healthier place. The first step, though, is knowing where you are now. Where are your roots planted? What are those unsupportive beliefs that aren't serving you well? If you're an Executive like Elizabeth, you might identify with many of these baloney beliefs:

▨ I am unsafe.

▨ I cannot just leave things up to chance.

▨ I have to know what's ahead so that I can prepare and protect everyone.

▨ People are undependable.

▨ I can handle it as long as I know what's coming.

▨ I can't ever let my guard down.

▨ I can't just trust others to keep my children safe.

▨ Most people are irresponsible.

▨ I have to be in charge so that nothing bad happens.

The Executive Contributors

You're probably thinking about where these baloney beliefs originated. How did they take hold? How did they end up coloring so much of your life? I'll touch on a few possibilities, though I invite you *not* to dwell on them. In the meantime, just know it could have been a variety of experiences—huge or tiny. As I said earlier, this anxiety style could have evolved from the experience of moving around a lot during your childhood, a tumultuous divorce, parents with mental health issues, or an alcoholic caregiver—any experiences where uncertainty and change left you with feelings of insecurity and discomfort (at the slightest level) or fear and anxiety (at a deeper level).

One of the Executive moms in my community, Katrina, remembers vividly the smells of the hospital when she visited her mother there as a mere toddler. For six months her mother moved in and out of the hospital, fighting a rare form of cancer. The pungent hospital odor filled her tiny toddler nose, loud beeping noises filled her tiny ears, and bustling adults rushed past her every time she visited her mother in the hospital. Katrina recalls many friends and family members, always positive and hopeful, assuring her and her big sister that their mom would be just fine very soon. And while she heard their words and saw their smiles, she felt in her bones that they were absolutely terrified.

Years later, as an adult, she always carried a first aid kit with her. She wasn't carrying it in case *she* needed it. No, she carried it in case someone else got hurt and needed to clean and dress any wounds right away. *We don't want anyone to get an infection and need to go to the hospital, right?* Planning ahead, being prepared, and helping to keep others safe (even strangers) is a common thread in Katrina's life to this day. She also shared that her big sister, only four years old at the age of their mother's fight with cancer, exhibits even more typically Executive tendencies. For instance, last Thanksgiving, Big Sis shared a nicely detailed spreadsheet with the family so that everyone could organize and plan out what to bring to their turkey dinner. Many moms have a big aha moment when they uncover the single childhood experience that most contributed to their anxiety style. Once they can connect the dots and better understand themselves, it's much easier to let go of the self-judgment (or shame) and move forward.

The Executive Triggers

So now what? How do you change a lifelong anxiety style so that it no longer controls you? How do you stop those negative patterns and start new, healthier habits? Let's start with situational triggers. These are the moments when your anxiety style is being actively engaged. If you can notice a trigger while it's happening, you'll be able to more purposely *respond* instead of *react* to the situation or event.

The first step is noticing when you've been triggered. I encourage you to take a moment, right now, to identify your most common triggers. These are typical situations, people, or phrases that leave you feeling more hurt or upset than feels "appropriate" for the situation. As you read the following list, circle the ones that particularly spark an emotional reaction in your body.

"We have to change our vacation plans again."
"Everything will be fine; don't worry about it."
"Congratulations on your new job and move across the country!"
"Let's do something different this Christmas."
"I have to reschedule our meeting tomorrow."
"Why do you have to control everything?"

Sometimes the same trigger will have a minor effect on you at one point but a huge impact on you at another point in time. Tolerance levels depend on your emotional fuel tank. Maybe you recently had a wonderful weekend with your family at your favorite mountain hideaway. At this point, you're feeling very safe and loved, appreciated, and connected with people. If your partner tells you his company just got bought out and there might be some big changes happening in the coming year, you might feel mildly concerned (your emotional tank is high). However, if you just had a difficult day at work and discovered your son's entire soccer season was canceled because of storm damage to the soccer fields, your husband's news may leave you feeling overpowered by anxiety and upset. (Your emotional tank is low, my friend.)

Understanding and acknowledging your triggers is an important key to insight and taking action. You can only help yourself if you *realize* that your anxieties are being triggered. When you find yourself suddenly flustered, stop and take a breath. In just a few more paragraphs and all through chapter 10, you'll learn special tools curated just for *you* to use in those triggered moments.

How Executives Flourish

Now comes the fun step. Remember, all anxiety styles have corresponding flourish types. As humans, we often focus on the threats in our environment and the negative characteristics we believe about ourselves. It's human nature. It's also especially common among moms. So let's highlight and celebrate all the areas where you shine! Consider where the very traits that have hurt you have also served you well.

What simple actions can you take to heal, grow, and become happier and less dependent on the moods, words, and actions of others? We're going to make a list of the good stuff. What skills have you developed by being an Executive like Elizabeth? What are you particularly good at, where others seem to struggle? This is the moment when your roots are firmly planted in healthy soil, the mist has cleared, *and* you've got a chilled water bottle and your favorite tunes playing in your earbuds. Let's embrace your Executive flourish type!

Let me ask you this, Momma:
Can you schedule out the next six months like nobody's business?

Do you take the time to read through all those e-mails from the kids' school?

Are you always more prepared than others for unanticipated events?

Are you more organized than most people?

Do you know where everything is at home and at work?

Are you one of the most dependable and responsible people you know?

Are you really good at communicating with friends and family when it comes to holiday plans or family trips?

Can you read people and situations really well?

Are you a kind and compassionate person?

Do coworkers and friends come to you for advice on organizing or planning?

Do you like these qualities about yourself? Do you value these characteristics? Do you feel proud of showing up in the world as a responsible, dependable, organized person who cares about the safety and security of your loved ones? Wouldn't you like to have more friends who have these same qualities? Do you agree that many people don't have these traits? You are amazing, my friend! Let's look at that list again. Now, from this place of gratitude and acknowledgment of your special skills, let's focus on what you can do to amplify the good aspects of this flourish type and minimize the areas where it's no longer serving you in your life.

The Executive's Life Lesson

What if your lesson in this life is **to feel emotionally safe regardless of what life might throw at you?** Maybe your biggest challenge is knowing you and your loved ones are safe and cared for no matter what. It's like wealthy people who grow up without money; they may continue to behave as if their millions could disappear at any moment because that underlying feeling of financial instability still feels real. Emotional security can work the same way. Are you truly as unsafe as you perceived you were when you were that child, without full understanding and without full control over your life? Maybe, just maybe, you are a millionaire now (emotionally speaking), but you're still behaving as if you're broke. While this lesson may not be learned overnight, you can begin now with this mantra: *I am safe now. I am the adult now. I am resilient and strong. I can totally handle this.* As entrepreneur and mom Cynthia Garcia reminded me when I interviewed her for my podcast, *Stretch Marks,* "You have survived every single thing that has happened to you thus far in your life." She's right. You've got this. You're stronger and more resilient than you give yourself credit for.

The first step is doing those things for yourself. Show yourself the acknowledgment, respect, and kindness you deserve. How can you show up for yourself *today*? What can you do at this moment? How can you more often check in with your emotions and see if there's a true cause for alarm or not? According to poet and author Kahlil Gibran, "Our anxiety does not come from thinking about the future, but from wanting to control it."

The Executive Self-Care Exercises and Tools

Here are the handpicked strategies for you, the Executive mom. Incorporating these tools will allow you to reduce feelings of stress and flusterment because they specifically balance out those areas where your anxiety style isn't supporting your needs. I've included strategies to use once a year, once a week, once daily, and five times a day. Before you roll your eyes and ask, "Who has time for all that?" these are simple strategies that you can make into habits by considering your motivational style from chapter 3. Start with just one of these strategies listed below—whichever one makes you smile or nod your head first. Once it's become a beneficial habit in your life, circle back to this page and start another strategy. Set a reminder, text a friend to be your accountability partner, or create a micro-goal out of it. Again, remember to use your personal motivational style to make it *easy.*

> *Knowing what to do means little if you don't actually do it.*

Once a Year: Emotional Strengths Check

Once each year, around your birthday or Mother's Day (or any other holiday that marks an important time for you), spend 30 minutes doing an Emotional Strengths Check. You'll want to walk or drive to a quiet park, beach, or hilltop. My clients enjoy doing this practice somewhere they don't go very often. Ideally, go somewhere where you'll be surrounded by nature. When you take yourself out of your normal environment, away from common distractions, and you immerse yourself in the fresh air and visual stimulation of a natural environment, your central nervous system will be more relaxed and your mind will be more likely to retain its focus on the task at hand. Grab a journal or notebook and free-write responses to the following questions. Note: I know you might be tempted to do this right now, at the end of an exhausting day, sitting in your bed or on your sofa next to the laundry pile. *Don't.*

Instead, make a date with yourself this week to drive or walk somewhere on your own for an hour. Then write out your responses to the following prompts (in the order given):

In this last year, I have successfully survived these difficulties/ challenges . . .

In this last year, I was most anxious about . . .

If I wasn't worried about _____ I could have . . . (Write 4–5 of these.)

I get most of my emotional support from . . .

I feel financially safe and secure when . . .

I feel physically safe and secure when . . .

In this last year, I felt so calm and happy in that moment when . . .

In this last year, I felt so proud of myself when . . .

Given what I've learned about myself in this last year, how will I show up for myself even more in the coming year?

Now, text or e-mail yourself whatever you wrote for the last prompt. Then add that to the Emergency Emotional Support Plan you'll create in chapter 10.

Once a Week: A New Hobby

The weekly practice I recommend for Executive moms is learning a new hobby that requires mental concentration and physical movement. Can you think of a fun practice or activity that you don't normally do? It should be something that takes you a bit out of your comfort zone and requires both your brain and your body, like knitting, hula hooping, or roller skating. Once every week, take 20 to 30 minutes (and you can do this with your kiddos, alone, or with friends) to try something new. Maybe spend that time relearning how to rollerblade. Or, learn how to play a ukulele, do cartwheels in the backyard, or practice yodeling.

You'll experience a playful self-kindness when trying something new that doesn't actively contribute to the well-being of your family. The expectations are low; you don't have to be good at it. If you're terrible at yodeling, who cares? Spending some time each week engaging in a fun and silly physical activity can help reduce your stress and anxiety. If you do it with your kids, you might find a unique opportunity for bonding. They'll see a different side of you that emerges when you're not good at something, when you're learning, and when you're being kind and lighthearted with yourself. What an incredible opportunity for your children to see that their caretaker can slow down, get into the present moment, and learn something new, right?

Once Daily: Avoiding Zombies

This strategy is particularly important when there is heightened conflict or turmoil on the planet. "Zombies" are people or content that is disturbing to deal with (or read about)—content that continues to eat away at you for the rest of the day. For hours after you absorb the upsetting information, your mind is distracted, your body is drained, and your mood is disheartened. The first step in avoiding zombies is self-awareness. Do you openly scroll on platforms that could surprise you with content you're not actively seeking or emotionally prepared for? Do you answer your phone when you know the person calling is likely to share loads of fearful or upsetting stories? Do you read the morning news regardless of your emotional state? Do you scroll Instagram regardless of how much you've slept or how much stress you're experiencing that day?

Knowing yourself and your current level of emotional resilience is key to protecting your mental health. You are in control, my friend. You get to choose if and when you are ready to absorb emotionally heavy or disturbing content. When you become more purposeful and protective of your emotional well-being, your children, your work, and your quality of life will benefit immensely.

Five Times a Day: The Five-Minute Fake Smile

I love neurohacks because they take very little time, energy, or money. They are simple too. I teach them because they are really good at reducing anxiety and refocusing attention on what matters most. A quarter of a century ago, when I was in college (holy moly, does that make me feel old!), I learned about the pencil smile study. Researchers had participants hold a pencil in their mouth either across their teeth so their "smile muscles" were activated, or straight out by pursing their lips around the circumference of the pencil so their "frown muscles" were activated. According to the study's results, people emulating a smile reported significantly more happiness and less stress than their frowning counterparts. This study has gone on to replicate its results in many shapes and forms over the last few decades. What we've learned is that our brains release the neurochemicals to match what our body is doing.

Link your fake smile to something you're already doing five times a day, like washing your hands or getting into your car. As B. J. Fogg suggests in his fabulous book, *Tiny Habits*, hook your new habit to a specific anchor. For instance, if you're linking your fake smile to washing your hands, the trigger or anchor would be turning on the water. If you're linking your fake smile strategy to getting into your car, your trigger could be clicking your seatbelt or hitting the ignition button. An anchor is a super-specific part of an activity you already do regularly.

---

*"Sometimes your joy is the source of your smile,
but sometimes your smile can be the source of your joy."*
—Zen master Thich Nhat Hanh

Let's Review

- You are more powerful when you know and notice your triggers.
- You can show self-love by articulating your needs effectively.
- You can show self-kindness by celebrating your superpowers.
- You can show self-value when using your self-care strategies.
- You are innately worthy of love, respect, attention, and affection.

The Four-Part Breath Mantra for Executive Moms

You can go to www.ambertrueblood.com/books to download a special guided meditation and mantra practice for Executive moms.

Sit quietly. Inhale deeply. Relax your shoulders. Exhale fully. Relax your jaw. Inhale deeply. Then say the following:

> *I am safe. (exhale)*
> *I am sound. (hold)*
> *I let go. (inhale)*
> *I am found. (hold)*
> *(repeat)*

8

THE FIGHTER ▲

ARE YOU A FIGHTER MOM? LET'S FIND OUT. Getting to know your primary anxiety style and flourish type will lead to more self-acceptance and self-kindness, less conflict with those you love, and a healthy way to navigate this life. If this is your type, this chapter will allow you to better understand yourself so you can have more of what you want in this life.

Remember Faith? She's the Fighter mom who truly values her independence and tenacity. She doesn't shy away from adversity or freeze in an emergency. Women like Faith generally feel energized and proud of their ability to survive despite trauma or big challenges. They often experience a lot of drama in their lives, both as children and as adults. For Faith, the most important things in the world are being able to protect those she loves and stand up for those who cannot stand up for themselves. If you're like Faith, you also feel an energetic high when you can show others how resilient and strong you are, emotionally and psychologically. On the inside, however, you may feel weak and less confident than what you present to the outside world.

You might develop this flourish type if you experienced trauma or turmoil in your childhood and were not protected by those who should have protected you. Often, Fighters learned at a young age how to fend for themselves. It could be that their parents were neglectful, narcissistic, or emotionally or physically abusive, leaving the child to fight for their own protection and survival. These experiences can lead to one's belief that they won't be protected or safe unless they are loud about their needs and stand up for themselves. Fighters were taught early on that depending on others was useless or even potentially dangerous.

As a result of her childhood experience, the Fighter mom's priorities, values, decisions, fears, perceptions, thoughts, behaviors, and beliefs are influenced by the deep drive to fight both for herself and for those she loves.

The Fighter mom is often drawn to situations and experiences that reinforce the label of "survivor." She's survived so much in her life that the idea of a life filled with ease can be very uncomfortable. Moms with this anxiety style are so accustomed to struggle that they often move subconsciously toward drama or difficulty even when they're exhausted and flustered.

Faith's anxiety style is like a filter that translates the perceptions of the world around her. Her experience of the people she meets, the challenges she faces, and the opportunities she's offered are all translated through this lens. When you're a Fighter, your decisions and emotions are fueled by a deep underlying desire to protect and stand up for those who need it. You are now the protector for others. You have become the person your younger self so needed and deserved. And that, my friend—while clearly commendable—is a lot to take on.

The Fighter Clues

If this is your anxiety style, you're likely to feel unsteady or untrusting when life is running smoothly. You might find yourself just waiting for the other shoe to drop. While calm, success, and happiness are goals, it can feel hard to let your guard down and actually enjoy yourself 100 percent when times are good.

Fighters may feel more energized and productive when there's a bad guy to fight, a challenge to overcome, or a cause to battle for (or against). In fact, you might find that when a challenge appears in your environment, you step forward while those around you step back (or even run away screaming). This is both wonderful and, well, sometimes not helpful to your life.

Do many of these clues resonate with you? Do you think of yourself as a survivor? Do you speak up and act even if you're scared or uncertain? Does your life seem to read like a movie? Let me tell you here and now, my friend: You can still wear the badge of "survivor" *and* learn how to embrace a life of ease and joy, a life where you feel safe to your core. You've developed this unique skill to protect yourself, and you've become accustomed to a life filled with crazy stories. And while that can feel exciting at times, it can also be draining, exhausting, and depleting. Like all five anxiety styles, you've developed these traits for good reason. They've allowed you to function with less anxiety and overwhelm in many areas of your life. Your anxiety style has allowed you to focus on what you value most. Because you highly value these connections in your life, with healthy habits your relationships flourish. As a Fighter, you've developed flourish traits that many others envy. Faith, for instance, often feels excited and energized when facing challenges at work or when a unforeseen roadblock pops into her life. She's also really good at noticing when others are struggling or in trauma. Faith seldom lets fear keep her from stepping in to help or rescue others from physical or emotional danger.

That's why we are not here to change who you are. No way. Instead, let's figure out the areas of this flourish type that serve you really well and celebrate those. Then we'll figure out what parts of your anxiety style no longer serve you, and we'll learn together how to release those. Last, you'll get new communication strategies to minimize your unhealthy cycles. You deserve peace and happiness. You're a Fighter baby, and that is flippin' phenomenal!

The Fighter Cycles

If you're still unsure about how this style applies to your life, let's touch on some common trends. You may have patterns of blowing up at work, changing jobs frequently, or moving from city to city. In your relationships, you might have a history of choosing partners who treat you like your parents (or caretakers) treated you. You might feel drawn to friends and romantic partners who are manipulative, emotionally labile, or who run hot and cold. This anxiety style might also affect your life in more subtle ways. You might take risks financially that put you in a vulnerable position, spark fights with friends, or find yourself in arguments with total strangers. While these experiences can often leave you energized and amped up, long periods in "survival mode" can really take their toll on your body and your emotional state. If you feel exhausted, you may benefit from using the strategies in this book to learn how to be comfortable amid the calm.

The Fighter's Baloney Beliefs

Understanding the "baloney beliefs" underlying your anxiety style can be challenging. While reading these might sting a bit, it's an important step in this process. By bringing these uncomfortable beliefs to the surface of your conscious mind, we can more easily dispel them—take the wind from their sails, so to speak. Baloney beliefs are the unsubstantiated, accidental beliefs you often don't even realize you hold. If you're a Fighter, let's take a moment to dredge up the baloney beliefs associated with this style. That way, we can start to dismantle them together.

Remember how you're a cashapona? If your roots (beliefs) are no longer serving you, if they're no longer supporting you or feeding you nutrient-rich soil or sufficient water, let's get you moving. You can grow strong, new roots by creating healthier beliefs that support you better.

Understanding exactly how you ended up rooted in this particular spot is less important than learning the skills to move to a healthier place. The first step, though, is knowing where you are now. Where are your roots planted? What are those unsupportive beliefs that aren't serving you well? Remember, "Not everything that weighs you down is yours to carry."

If you're a Fighter like Faith, you may identify with many of these baloney beliefs:

- ▲ I always seem to live in struggle.
- ▲ I'm valuable because I'm a Fighter.
- ▲ I can only depend on myself.
- ▲ People like me because I'm strong.
- ▲ I have to fight to get the life I want.

▲ Nothing worthwhile is easy.

▲ Easy is boring.

▲ I can save, help, or rescue anyone and everyone.

▲ Nobody else will fight for me.

▲ If life feels simple or easy, it's only temporary.

The Fighter Contributors

You're probably thinking about where these beliefs originated. How did they take hold? How did they end up coloring so much of your life? I'll touch on a few possibilities, though I invite you *not* to dwell on them. In the meantime, just know they could have been a variety of experiences—huge or tiny. There's a good chance that your baloney beliefs came from what you were taught as a child. The experiences you had in your youth showed you, plain as day, that if you needed to feel safe and get what you wanted in this life, you had only yourself to depend on. If you wanted love, you'd have to fight for it. If you wanted attention, safety, or acknowledgment, you would speak up for yourself, even if that meant making others uncomfortable. These beliefs helped you to survive and even thrive as a child, and probably into adulthood as well. Now it's time to look at these beliefs and drop those that are no longer serving you.

One of the Fighter moms in my community, Naomi, recounts vividly the scene of her five-year-old self sitting on the couch with her mom and older sister as her drunk and yelling father pointed a gun at the three of them. That particular ordeal ended without any physical injuries. Afterward, everyone simply went to bed, and the event was never addressed or mentioned again by anyone in the family. Chaos and danger were the baseline, the *normal* way of life, in her childhood home. Naomi remembers sitting in her little Playskool plastic desk, eating an Oreo cookie, and playing with an Etch A Sketch as a screaming fight between her siblings and parents barreled over and around her—objects flying and tempers soaring. She describes herself as very calm in that moment, like the eye of a hurricane.

Now, as an adult, she still feels very calm amid chaos and drama. In fact, when her life is going well, she literally feels sick to her stomach. Perhaps it's the anticipation, the not knowing what bad thing might happen next, that feels even worse than experiencing the bad thing. Naomi has learned over the years, through lots of emotional work, how to avoid the people and situations where major physical and emotional harm is likely to happen. She's still continuing to learn how to enjoy the moments of calm "before the storm" instead of fearing them. Maybe the storm isn't coming. Maybe, just maybe, it's now safe for Fighter moms like Naomi to let go and cruise, relax, and enjoy the life they've created. Many moms have a big aha moment when they uncover the single childhood experience that most contributed to their anxiety style. Once they can connect the dots and better understand themselves, it's much easier to let go of the self-judgment (or shame) and move forward.

The Fighter Triggers

So now what? How do you change a lifelong anxiety style so that it no longer controls you? How do you stop those negative patterns and start new, healthier habits? Let's start with situational triggers. These are the moments when your anxiety is being actively engaged. If you can notice a trigger while it's happening, you'll be able to more purposely *respond* instead of *react* to the situation or event.

The first step is noticing when you're being triggered. I encourage you to take a moment, right now, to identify your most common triggers. These are typical situations, people, or phrases that leave you feeling more hurt or upset than feels "appropriate" for the situation. As you read the following list, circle the ones that particularly spark an emotional reaction in your body.

Your relationship is calm, and everyone is getting along well.
Your job is going well, and you feel appreciated and respected.
Your money situation is improving slowly and steadily.
Your friends care about you, support you, and acknowledge you.

These might seem strange for "triggers." Unlike for the other anxiety styles, your triggers are stability, calm, and ease. These triggers feel uncomfortable and unfamiliar, whereas drama and trauma and challenge, that's where you know your place. That is where you shine. That is where you know what to say and do to protect yourself and those you love. What if you could actually get to a place where you could be comfortable in the ease? What if you could truly enjoy it, embrace it, and live it?

Recently, Naomi felt triggered after a particularly pleasant and fun evening with girlfriends. Feeling sick to her stomach, she described a pressure building up and moving into her chest. It's as if Naomi grew up high in the Himalayan mountains. Her body acclimated to the low amount of oxygen that only people raised in very high altitudes can withstand. Most of us would feel nauseated and headachy at that height. But not Naomi. She spent years in that environment, and every part of her physiology has learned how to thrive despite the harsh conditions. Now though, as an adult living at sea level, her body hasn't yet fully adjusted to the higher levels of oxygen, the warmer climate, or the calmer winds. She sometimes even finds herself metaphorically holding her breath, re-creating part of the hostile environment of her youth, so that her body can fall back into a state of calm more easily.

Understanding and acknowledging your triggers is an important key to insight and taking action. You can only help yourself if you *realize* that your anxieties are being triggered. When you find yourself suddenly flustered, stop and take a breath. In just a few more paragraphs and all through chapter 10, you'll learn special tools curated just for *you* to use in those triggered moments.

How Fighters Flourish

Now comes the fun step. Remember, all anxiety styles have a corresponding flourish types. As humans, we often focus on the threats in our environment and the negative characteristics we believe about ourselves, and Fighters can be particularly hard on themselves. So let's highlight and celebrate all the areas where you shine! Consider where the very traits that have hurt you have also served you well.

What simple actions can you take to heal, grow, and become happier and less dependent on the moods, words, and actions of others? We're going to make a list of the good stuff. What skills have you developed by being a Fighter like Faith? What are you particularly good at, where others seem to struggle? This is the moment when your roots are firmly planted in healthy soil, the mist has cleared, *and* you've got on the best hiking gear and coolest sunglasses. Let's embrace your Fighter traits!

> **Let me ask you this, Momma:**
> Do you often stand up to bullies?
> Are you a loyal and trustworthy friend?
> Do you go out of your way to help those in a crisis?
> Do you feel energized and amped up when facing a challenge in your life?
> Do you just seem to know when people are victims of trauma and need your help?
> Are you able to speak up for yourself when you need to?
> Are you transparent and honest?
> Are you responsible and respectful of others' feelings?

Do you like these qualities about yourself? Do you value these characteristics? Do you feel proud of showing up in the world as an honest, trustworthy, responsible, loyal friend? Wouldn't you like to have more friends who have these same qualities? Do you agree that many people don't have these traits?

You are amazing, my friend! Look at that list again. From this place of gratitude and acknowledgment of your special skills, let's focus on what you can actually do to amplify the good and minimize any anxiety aspects of this flourish type.

The Fighter's Life Lesson

What if your lesson in this life is to finally be able to **stop surviving your life, fighting every battle that comes your way, and begin living your life?** Olympian Jackie Joyner-Kersee once said, "If I stop to kick every barking dog, I am not going to get where I'm going." Now, I don't think she was talking about literally hurting animals, but I think you get her point. What if you could truly enjoy the lulls between the mayhem and stop waiting for the other shoe to drop? What if not every battle you see is yours to fight? What if you drew into your life more stability, consistency, safety, and calm—and it didn't feel boring to you? What if you drew people into your life who you could truly trust to stand up for you, to protect you, to be there for you no matter what? How would that feel? Maybe your biggest challenge is letting go of your "survivor" title and graduating, finally, into a life of ease, comfort, and love.

The Fighter Self-Care Exercises and Tools

Here are the handpicked strategies for you, the Fighter mom. Incorporating these tools will allow you to reduce feelings of stress and anxiety because they specifically balance out those areas where your anxiety style isn't supporting your needs. I've included strategies to use once a year, once a week, once daily, and five times a day. Before you roll your eyes and ask, "Who has time for all that?" these are simple strategies that you can make into habits by considering your motivational style from chapter 3. Start with just *one* of these strategies—whichever one makes you smile or nod your head first. Once it's become a beneficial habit in your life, circle back to this page and start another strategy. Set a reminder, text a friend to be your accountability partner, or create a micro-goal out of it. Again, remember to use your personal motivational style to make it *easy*.

> *Knowing what to do means little*
> *if you don't actually do it.*

Once a Year: My True Value Exercise

Take a few minutes, once a year, to write out in your journal all the qualities and traits you value about yourself. Focus on those related not only to your survivor superhero characteristics, but also to your non-survivor qualities. Write down all the people in your life who value and respect you, and spend a few minutes feeling gratitude for those people. If you don't have any or many in that category, begin a visualization practice where you imagine what life would look like surrounded by people you could trust to care for you, love you, and protect you, no matter what. Imagine what they would say, what they might do, and what it will feel like once those people are drawn into your life. This is powerful work, but it requires consistency. So you'll want to couple the five-times-a-day practice later in this chapter with this exercise. Make sure the daily mantra you chose aligns with your journal entry.

Once a Week: Checking In — The Ask

This is a weekly self-awareness practice where you ask yourself a question: *Where in my life am I making things more difficult than they need to be?* Be quiet and let the answer bubble up inside you. Take a walk or a shower, and let the question linger for a bit. Then write the question out in your journal and see what comes up. If you make this a regular weekly practice, you're far more likely to be aware of your choices and patterns. Once you answer this question, you can then decide that either *yes, this is a battle or challenge I consciously want to take part in*, or *no, I'm going to pass on this and not get myself involved in it. I will not allow it to disrupt my life, my health, my children, my relationship, or my job.* By asking yourself this weekly question, you gain control over your triggers. You get to decide what battles you want to fight, which ones you care about, and when you have the energy and bandwidth to take them on. The cycle of drama and difficulty then becomes a conscious choice instead of a reflexive, automatic cycle. You become the boss.

Once Daily: Qigong Breathing Exercise

Qigong is an ancient breathwork practice focused on using body, mind, and breath to improve and support mental well-being. There are several different types of qigong, just like there are multiple meditation practices. They are often used to reduce stress, modulate pain, and increase energy in the body. I recommend taking your time and doing a bit of research before you jump into a qigong practice. One of my private clients found so much relief in this type of breathwork that she became certified to teach others the practice.

Five Times a Day: Mantra Practice

Choose one of the following mantras and say it five times every day. I recommend linking the practice to something you already do several times throughout your day. For instance, say it every time you wash your hands, see the number 7 on the clock, or notice someone wearing your favorite color. Relax your shoulders, listen to the words as you speak them, and pay attention to your thoughts. If the following mantras feel like too big of a reach, create your own mantra, framing it as "Every day I feel a bit more like . . ." or "I am working toward feeling like . . ."

Example mantras:
"I deserve a life of ease, surrounded by people who love, respect, and protect me."
"I am valuable and lovable for who I am, not what I do."
"I am ready to replace struggle with joy and ease."

Let's Review

▲ You are more powerful when you know and notice your triggers.
▲ You can show self-love by articulating your needs effectively.
▲ You can show self-kindness by celebrating your flourish type.
▲ You can show self-value when using your self-care strategies.
▲ You are innately worthy of love, respect, attention, and protection.

The Four-Part Breath Mantra for Fighter Moms

You can go to www.ambertrueblood.com/books to download a special guided meditation and mantra practice for Fighter moms.

Sit quietly. Inhale deeply. Relax your shoulders. Exhale fully. Relax your jaw. Inhale deeply. Then say the following:

> *I am worthy. (exhale)*
> *I am safe. (hold)*
> *I hold myself (inhale)*
> *with ease and grace. (hold)*
> *(repeat)*

PART III

FLOURISHING

9

KNOWING YOURSELF

WELCOME TO MY FAVORITE PART! This is where you get to really take the reins. You're in charge of your own emotional health and wellness. Of course, no matter how much you're thriving, life likes to throw challenges your way. Let's get you ready to move from reacting and surviving to responding and thriving.

In the next chapter, you'll create your own Emergency Emotional Support Plan (EESP). You'll determine your best course of action and learn how to implement it when you most need it. But, before you can implement anything to reduce your anxiety or eliminate your fluster, you have to be *aware* of when you need the help. Often, there's a trigger sign, a symptom, an indication that your emotions are running you instead of the other way around. Yes, sometimes you clearly know your anxiety has been triggered. It's obvious to you and everyone within a mile radius. Other times, you don't even realize you've been triggered until much later. The sooner you can recognize you're having an amplified emotional response, the sooner you can determine what you need most at that moment. Our logical mind doesn't necessarily think clearly when we're exhausted or flustered. Part III of this book is all about choosing your most powerful strategies and tools ahead of time. Then when you notice your emotional state is triggered, you'll know exactly what to do about it.

Knowing the Common Trigger Signs

The first step is knowing your personal trigger signs. Check out the following list and ask yourself, *What are the three most common trigger signs for me?* Even better, add your own if none of these apply. When you notice yourself nodding your head, smiling, or talking to yourself, that's the one you'll want to circle!

I start to cry or tear up easily.

I reach for a drink (earlier in the day or more often than normal).

I start snapping at the kids for little things (again, more than normal).

I find myself gritting or grinding my teeth at night.

I post something snarky or vent angrily on Facebook.

I call or text a certain friend to complain or vent.

I stop talking to my partner.

I get really quiet.

I start baking a pie (or making sourdough bread or a frittata).

I throw myself into my work.

I get a migraine.

I start shopping for stuff online that I don't need. (Ask yourself which website you go to most when you're in this mode.)

I dig into the freezer and eat all the ice cream I can find.

I start gambling or making rash financial decisions.

I spend hours playing online games.

I get really lethargic and either take a nap or go to bed early.

I lose my voice.

I distract myself with a new Netflix binge.

I start researching trips or vacations.

I look up divorce attorneys on the Internet.

I don't want to get out of my pajamas.

I start a big cleaning project.

I dole out harsher punishments than normal.

I stop eating, or I start overeating.

I pick fights with my sister or my partner.
My back goes out.

_____.

_____.

Circle three trigger signs and then make them even more specific if possible. (Write them out in your journal or in the margins on this page.) For instance, if you go to Overstock.com whenever you're upset, or reach out to a *certain* friend, or always begin cleaning out the garage, *that's* what I want you to write. For instance, when Daisy is particularly anxious, she scrolls Facebook and then comments passionately on random posts she'd never normally notice. When Elizabeth feels anxious, she suddenly cannot stand the level of mess in her house and begins a big project like reorganizing the hall closet. Our Fighter mom Faith goes straight to Tripadvisor and escapes by mentally planning a big adventurous trip. When Victoria feels anxious, she opens another bottle of wine. Our Lover mom Lisa digs into the mint chip ice cream as soon as the kids fall asleep.

Knowing your trigger responses will allow you to implement the strategies and practices that are going to help you sooner. Not only that, you'll also be far less likely to start an unnecessary argument or do something you'll regret later. Instead of making things worse, you can turn it all around much more quickly and easily. When you're tuned in and self-aware, you have a much better chance of doing something about your triggers.

Understanding Self-Care

Let's make something else very clear. The unfluster strategies you're learning in this book also serve as self-care strategies. However, there's a difference between true self-care and surface self-care. *True* self-care is any activity or practice that creates joy *and* increases your emotional bank account. It refuels you. It doesn't always look like some sort of luxurious experience, though. For me, as a Dynamo, I feel most emotionally refueled when I take time to accomplish or make significant progress on a project that is very important to me. When I do that, I am much less irritable and significantly less flusterable for the remainder of the day.

If you're a Lover mom, true self-care might involve a hike with your best friend, a romantic dinner with your partner, or a long talk on the phone with your mother. If you're an Executive mom, true self-care might be an entire afternoon in an empty house, or music playing while you clean out and reorganize your garage. If you're a Visionary mom, true self-care might look like a retreat or workshop with other visionaries where you can connect and share your dream plans. If you're a Fighter mom, true self-care might involve signing up for a sprint marathon or a weekend trip to somewhere you've never been (and where you don't know the language). True self-care is tuning into what drives you, what types of activities leave you feeling a burst of energy, a *high* so to speak. When you spend your time in these types of activities, you raise your baseline level of emotional resiliency. Increased emotional resiliency means that you're less likely to get anxious, agitated, impatient, frustrated, or flustered.

Let me ask you this: How often have you returned home after a pedicure or other relaxing activity to find the house even more of a disaster than when you left and everyone arguing? The temporary calm and joy you felt during your foot massage immediately dissolved as soon as you stepped through the door, right? That's a great indication that your self-care was *surface* self-care. It's easy to confuse surface self-care with true self-care because they both feel good in the moment. With surface self-care, when it's over, we often feel even more frustrated or irritable than we felt beforehand. Our assumption is that the pedicure filled our emotional bank account, but it didn't. It was nice while it lasted, but it only scraped the surface. It made us feel relaxed or excited or joyful only *during* the experience. It also raised our expectation that we *should* feel better afterward. So when we don't, our frustration is even more exacerbated. True self-care bolsters you in a much more profound way, and the effects last longer. And as we saw with our star moms, it doesn't look the same for everyone.

> *True self-care often comes in a shape*
> *we don't typically think of as self-care.*

It's important to remember the differences between true and surface self-care. You're going to choose three true self-care activities that you know refuel you deeply—even if people around you might think they sound crazy.

True Self-Care
- Provides **lasting** effects that refuel you emotionally and physically for longer than the time you're actually doing the activity.
- Creates a **deep** positive shift when done regularly. This practice energizes and allows you to feel more relaxed, flexible, forgiving, appreciative, and compassionate with yourself and others.
- Becomes a **habit** easily. Because of the lasting effects and deep benefits, true self-care becomes self-reinforcing very quickly.

Surface Self-Care
- Feels great **while** you're doing it.
- Can actually lead you to feel **less** calm and **more** irritable in the long run.
- May be an activity that is refueling to *others*, but not to **you**.
- Can feel more like an **obligation** than a fun, interesting, or exciting activity.

If you're not sure what true self-care is for you, ask yourself: What is something you don't do regularly (or at all), but when you did it in the past, it made you feel excited and energized, and—most important— shifted the current challenges in your life from daunting to doable? What is an activity you used to do that you loved, but you stopped doing because of life responsibilities, changed circumstances, or a baloney belief that you're too old or too out of shape?

Now, take a moment and jot down two or three true self-care activities that work for you. Do you feel deeply refueled when you go to the beach by yourself for an hour? When you take two hours to plan out the month in detail, with no interruptions? When you go for a long run in the hills with your best friend? When you clear a Saturday afternoon to work on a passion project? When you dance, do Pilates, meditate, or take a Yin Yoga class? Ideally, write down these activities in a journal.

Add big colored stars and fireworks around them. I want you to make it easy to find the page you've written them on. Don't have any experience with journaling? I can help with that.

20/80 Journaling

Journaling is a fantastic way to vent negative energy, get clarity, and figure out what you need most in that moment. However, be careful not to spend *all* of your journal time complaining or reliving the frustrations of your day. That is *not* particularly healthy or useful. I recommend you spend 20 percent of your journaling on venting or getting out all the dirty laundry. Then spend the remaining 80 percent either on gratitude for what you love and appreciate about your life or on imagining what you would like more of in your life. Draw a line across the page, about 20 percent of the way down, and vent only until you hit that line. Use the remainder of the page to write about what you want more of. Try not to use this time for planning or for figuring out "the how." Instead, focus on how you want to feel and what is most important to you.

"What you focus on grows. What you concentrate on is what you see more of in your life."
—Robin S. Sharma

One of my issues with self-help books is that many offer a one-size-fits-all solution. Unless that size is yours, we often end up setting ourselves up for disappointment and frustration. Instead, I encourage you to use your flourish type and your motivational style to better understand the strengths, talents, and opportunities for growth that are unique to *you*. Another tool I love for customizing your emotional wellness toolbox is SuperSenses. Use these to create even more specific powerful strategies to replace a flustered mom life with a life where you can truly flourish.

SuperSenses

Most of us have five functioning senses that receive input from the outside world. However, these senses aren't weighted equally. We don't necessarily pay the same amount of attention to what we *see* as what we *smell* or *taste*. Everyone is different. And many of us have one sense, a SuperSense, that tends to dominate our perception. Maybe you're more sensitive to sound than those around you. Maybe you're more reactive to smells than the rest of your family. Maybe you notice things in your visual field that most people do not.

Think of the language you use when you speak to people. Are you more likely to say, "I *think* I get what you're saying," "I *see* what you mean," "I *feel* you," or "I *hear* you"? (I don't think I've ever heard of someone saying "I *smell* what you mean." But you can see where I'm going with this.) We tend to use language that relates to our SuperSense. Once you identify your SuperSense, you can use it to your advantage. You can choose a self-care strategy that's particularly powerful for you because it's based on your SuperSense. The cool thing about this concept is that it's powerful not only for reducing mom fluster but also for amping up your mood and energy level when you need a boost. SuperSense strategies can both calm your nervous system and boost your energy levels when needed.

Here's how it works: When you want to reduce your feelings of frustration or overwhelm, you'll *minimize* the input to your SuperSense. When you want to improve your mood and increase your energy level, you'll selectively amplify the input to your SuperSense. I'll break it down by each sense.

If You're a Visual SuperSenser

When you're flustered:
- Cover the laundry pile with a neutral-colored blanket.
- Take any pile of papers that has been sitting out for more than two weeks and put it in a drawer or a box out of sight.
- Choose one counter or table in your home and spend 10 minutes clearing it and wiping it clean every morning.

- Make your bed.
- Temporarily remove colorful pillows, artwork, and knickknacks from view.

When you want a boost:
- Step outside and look up at the trees and sky (any nature around you).
- Google image search your favorite tourist destination and peruse the photos.
- Look through old photo albums or "moments" on your Facebook page.
- Spend a few minutes watching waves, a running stream, or ripples on a lake if you live near any bodies of water.
- Look through architecture or home magazines you find beautiful.
- Spread the joy to other Visual SuperSensers by posting a picture of your favorite place with the hashtag #unflusteredmom.

If You're an Auditory SuperSenser

When you're flustered:
- Use earplugs or headphones in your work space, bedroom, and kitchen (or wherever unwelcome noises are most likely to occur).
- Use a white noise app on your phone to drown out loud or sudden noises.
- Try zero-tech options like Flare Audio Calmer earplugs to reduce certain frequencies.

When you want a boost:
- Create or borrow two playlists: one for when you want to calm down and relax your nervous system, and another for when you want to amp up and energize your nervous system.
- Listen to music you loved between the ages of 14 and 24.
- Call a friend whose voice always engages and soothes you.
- Spread the joy to other Auditory SuperSensers by sharing your favorite uplifting song online with the hashtag #unflusteredmom.

If You're a SuperSmeller

When you're flustered:
- Keep the windows open or fans on in your home (and the bathroom door closed).
- Clean the stove often to minimize the chances of burning something unwanted and creating nasty smells.
- Teach the kids how to wash their own laundry as early as possible. (I recommend a step stool for a top-loading washer.)

When you want a boost:
- Order a few of your favorite essential oil scents to keep beside your bed, in the kitchen, in the car, and in your work space.
- Use candles or creams with your favorite scent to help elicit a calming sensation for your nervous system.
- Close your eyes and take three slow, deep breaths when you detect a smell you love, such as your morning coffee, the sweet scent of a pastry, or the flowers blooming outside. (Literally, stop and smell the flowers.)
- Spread the joy to other SuperSmellers by sharing your favorite hand cream, candles, or essential oils with the hashtag #unflusteredmom.

If You're a Tactile SuperSenser

When you're flustered:
- Cut the tags off your clothes.
- Wear 100 percent cotton (for any clothing that touches your skin).
- Wash your bedsheets more frequently to eliminate any sand or crumbs. (I'm not the only one with sand and crumbs in my bed, am I?)
- Notice your sensitivity to temperature fluctuations and dress in layers so you're always comfortable.

When you want a boost:
- Find a favorite sweater or scarf and lay it over your office chair.
- Spend 10 minutes petting your cat or dog (or borrow a neighbor's pet).

- Find a tactile talisman like a smooth stone or small furry stuffed animal to rub or hold between your fingers throughout the day.
- Spread the joy to other Tactile SuperSensers by posting a picture of your cozy socks or sweater with the hashtag #unflusteredmom.

If You're a SuperTaster

When you're flustered:
- Keep packets of your favorite flavor of gum or mints nearby at all times.
- Brush your teeth or use mouthwash throughout your day, particularly after meals and snacks.
- Drink lots of water.

When you want a boost:
- Have your favorite teas or coffee creamers on hand.
- Every week, plan to make, order in, or go out for a particularly delicious meal.
- Keep your go-to flavors (garlic, Himalayan salt, turmeric, etc.) in the kitchen to add an extra kick to meals and snacks.
- Spread the joy to other SuperTasters by posting a picture of your favorite dessert or meal with the hashtag #unflusteredmom.

Now you have another important tool in your emotional satchel. You can proactively notice and then modulate (which is just a fancy word for *control*) your sensory input to unfluster yourself.

What *Not* to Do

Before we move on to mindfulness and those awful "shoulds" we moms carry around like rock-filled grocery bags, I want to share what *not* to do. When feeling worn out and overwhelmed, there are a few common responses that many flustered moms turn to in hopes of feeling better. We vent to certain friends, we scan online posts and articles, we decide to start a big home project, we go on a juice fast, or we bake three boxes of brownie mix. Although these attempts may feel good in the moment, they are undoubtedly unhelpful in the long run.

Don't Hang Out with Vampires

Vampires are friends, colleagues, or neighbors who leave you feeling emotionally drained. Even if you adore them, they leave you feeling spent. If you live with vampires, this will be trickier. Try this: when a vampire is venting to you about something emotionally dark or disturbing, imagine bricks made of clear ice, glowing with light, stacking up around you. This is your energetically protective shield. You can learn to hear the vampire and be supportive without absorbing the torrent of negativity or hostility flying about the room. If you don't live with vampires, minimize your time with friends or extended family members who leave you feeling drained. This is particularly important when your emotional bank account is already on low. If it is low, and you see that your upcoming schedule that week includes some vampires, take action and cancel or postpone anything you can.

Don't Play with Zombies

You know when you read something awful, and it just eats away at you the rest of the day? That's zombie content. Zombies can be people, disturbing articles, social media platforms, or websites that feed off your brain matter. You just can't stop thinking about them. They make you feel sick to your stomach. Obviously, it's not benefiting you emotionally to hold that sort of content in your mind all day. It's also not helping those who are in the disturbing situation for you to be distracted all day or stay up all night stressing about it. When you're already in a flustered state, avoiding zombie content will keep you from digging yourself further into an emotional abyss.

Don't Start Something New

When you're feeling stressed, anxious, or emotionally drained, *do not* start something new. This is not the time to begin a new diet, change your medication, or spontaneously decide to remodel your bathroom. Instead, make sure you're eating healthful foods that make you feel energized and strong. Make sure you're drinking lots of water and getting good quality sleep. (In the next chapter, we'll dive into strategies to improve and protect

your sleep.) In the meantime, give your emotional well-being the foundation it needs with sleep, food, and water instead of giving your mind and
body new challenges to manage. Note: If you know from previous personal
experience that changing your diet or medication will, in fact, support you
emotionally, then by all means, go for it! Otherwise, tune in and uplevel
your basic physical needs: healthful food, quality sleep, and lots of water.

Don't Deplete Your Emotional Bank Account

The amount of emotional reserves you hold at any given time varies.
Some days you're feeling strong and emotionally resilient. Other days,
a dog food commercial has you reaching for the tissue box. When your
emotional bank account is low, focus on the strategies that will refill it
instead of letting it plummet all the way to zero. When you allow your
emotional bank account to get too low, it's far more likely you'll have a
big blowout with your partner, lose your patience with the kids, eat an
entire pint of ice cream, or finish that bottle of chardonnay by yourself.
Instead, notice when your emotional reserves are low (by remembering
the common trigger signs you checked off at the beginning of this chapter). Then go straight to the strategies on your EESP. Don't worry, the
majority of chapter 10 is devoted to your personalized EESP.

Don't Fall into a Social Media Hole

We all know what it's like to be distracted by Instagram or YouTube
videos. We call it "relaxing" or "taking a break." Is it really, though? I
don't love the idea of letting "the algorithm" decide what I should or
should not see today. You see, the magical algorithm's purpose is not to
keep you *happy* or *healthy*; it's to keep you *engaged*. Its job is to keep you
clicking and scrolling and reading and watching and clicking and scrolling and reading and watching—regardless of the content. Regardless of
your emotional well-being. Regardless of your worldly responsibilities.

In fact, research has taught these companies that our Neanderthal
brains are wired to disproportionately attend to the more disturbing,
more alarming content. Your attempt to "relax" could very well be
hijacked by the algorithm. So unless you are actively and purposefully

choosing every article you read and every video you watch, you're leaving your emotional health in the hands of a computer program. Until you resist the passive consumption of whatever the platform decides to show you next, it's very likely your nervous system will be activated negatively during your "relaxing break."

Instead, try turning off your phone or placing it in another room. You can retrain your brain to notice your surroundings. You can calm your central nervous system by focusing on nature more than human-made objects. You can model to your children what it's like to have truly focused interactions with other humans in your life. When you're off social media, you can more easily discover new ways to connect deeply with loved ones. Taking a break from your phone can also help you better notice how much time you were actually spending on it. Do you keep reaching for your phone at every stoplight? Do you take it into the bathroom, even at home? Do you feel uncomfortable when you don't know where it is? Do your notifications beep at you during dinner or chats with friends? Are the apps driving your life, or are *you* in charge? When you spend a few days away from the notifications, alerts, beeps, and chirps, you'll be able to take charge of your time and attention much more consciously. There's a scene in season eight of *The Office* where Ryan goes to a trivia night with his coworkers in hopes of winning the cash prize.

> *Host: You can't check smartphones during trivia, it's against the rules.*
> Ryan: Okay, I'm turning it off.
> *Host: Okay, you're not turning it off.*
> Ryan: I won't look at it.
> *Host: Sir?*
> Ryan: I can't—I can't not touch it.
> *Host: Okay, then we're going to have to take it away.*
> Ryan: Look, I can't, I can't not have my phone. I'm sorry.
> I want to be with my phone.

I know you want to be with your phone. I get it. I do too. But we can turn off our notifications, delete the apps that don't serve our mental health, and give ourselves breaks more often. From a parenting perspective, the effects of social media on your child's brain and on their central nervous system is no joke. Learning how to better control it yourself, is the first step. It's tricky to expect our children, with underdeveloped prefrontal cortexes, to handle the highly addictive realm of technology when many of us have difficulty with it. (I'll describe how to do this with your kids in my next book, *The Trueblood Method: How to Raise Kind, Creative, Compassionate, and Resilient Children in Today's World.*)

Daily Mindfulness

Many of the self-care strategies listed in this book are effective in reducing anxiety because they foster a state of increased mindfulness. Becoming mindful in the moment takes our attention away from the guilt about yesterday's snarky comment, the shame of the awful boyfriend you had in your 20s, the anxiety about tomorrow, and the fear of the unknown future. Focusing your mind on what is happening right now is the most foolproof way to unfluster yourself physiologically and psychologically. Use the following strategies to easily wend mindfulness into your busy daily life:

The Waiting Game

When working, traveling, or driving, you often spend a lot of time waiting. Use these moments waiting in line or waiting on the phone to get mindful. If you're outside, try to notice the slightest sound you can hear, the smallest leaf or stone you can see, and the subtlest smell you can detect. Tuning into the environment around you can calm your mind and reconnect you to your body in the present moment.

Numbers on the Clock

When you're on the go, a simple way to incorporate mindfulness is to choose a number (like 7). Any time you look at the clock and the time includes the number 7, take a moment to get mindful. For instance, when you notice it's 9:27 AM, take three slow, deep breaths. Close your eyes and feel the air slowly entering and leaving your body.

Plan on It

Most of us keep track of our priorities and tasks by using a digital to-do list, a paper calendar, or a productivity app. Make sure that at least one item on your daily list is an unplugged activity that replenishes you emotionally, mentally, or spiritually—for instance, a mindfulness shower, a coffee-walk, or a yoga practice. If you don't have time for these, choose one of the one-minute strategies in the next chapter.

The Mantra Focus

Flusterment and frustration result when our precious time, energy, and resources are not aligned with what we value. Maintaining your focus as a mom is virtually impossible in this world of constant distraction and demands for our attention. Mantras can remind you what you value most at this point in your life. They help keep you pointed in the "right" direction. I recommend using mantras or affirmations three to four times each day as a reminder and inspiration to realign and refocus your limited time and energy. Mantras work best when kept consistent for at least a few weeks.

You'll want to choose a mantra that

you can remember easily,
highlights what is truly important to you, and
feels like a reach goal (but not an impossible goal).

For instance, your mantra might be "I'm so grateful my loved ones are happy, healthy, safe, and together," or "I feel surrounded by support, kindness, inspiration, and calm every day." Bonus tip: Link your mantra practice to an activity you already do three to four times each day. For example, say your mantra each time you drink water, park your car, or put on lip balm. Remember, when we link a new habit to an established activity, we are far more likely to keep it up.

How *Shoulds* Hurt Us

Shoulds are terrible. They hurt us because they lie, distract us, and discourage us. How do *shoulds* lie? Well, when you've internalized a *should* in your life, whether it's about your career, your weight, your role, or your relationships, it's seldom based on truth. As moms, we often assume the best about others and the worst about ourselves. Of course, social media feeds, films, and TV shows do not help us create realistic expectations for our lives. *I shouldn't have any lines on my forehead.* Our *shoulds* are based on our perceptions of what other people have, what they're doing, or what they look like. Unfortunately, these perceptions of other people are rarely true. My husband worked in the entertainment industry his entire career and often told me stories of how famously gorgeous and perfect actresses looked *before* the team of hairstylists and makeup artists and costume and lighting crew got involved. It. Isn't. Real.

How often do you judge yourself for not living up to a standard or goal that *isn't even real*? When we do this, our confidence can plummet, shame jumps in, and symptoms of depression and anxiety can flourish.

How do *shoulds* distract us? Well, how often do you pause your self-judgment long enough to figure out if the *should* is based on something *you* truly want and value? Uncovering the author behind your *should* is a valuable first step to dismantling the potentially negative impact of *shoulding* yourself. For instance, if you realize "I should never miss bedtime with my kids" is based on your mother-in-law's values, then you can ask yourself how *you* feel about it. Maybe walking your kids to school is much more important to you than bedtime. *Shoulds* are so incredibly ingrained and subtle that they can easily distract you from figuring out how *you* truly feel about them. The next time you're feeling self-judgment or guilt, ask yourself, *Is this my value or someone else's value?*

How do *shoulds* discourage us? Self-judgment seldom helps to motivate us. When we live in a world of comparison and *shoulds*, we end up feeling jealous, resentful, or disillusioned. Or all three. These emotional responses deplete our energy and our ability to be emotionally resilient. Instead of focusing on yourself and the good you can do for yourself, the focus shifts to *others*. Since you have no control over the actions or behavior of others, you're left as either a victim or an observer. Instead, release the *shoulds* by asking yourself, "Is this truly important to me, and why?"

What You've Learned About Taking Care of *You*

- You know your top three trigger signs.
- You know the three true self-care practices that work best for you.
- You can use your SuperSense to unfluster yourself.
- You know what *not* to do.
- You know how to easily become more mindful every day.
- You know how to search for the author of the *shoulds* that pop up in your life.

10

CREATING YOUR PLAN

THIS CHAPTER IS ALL ABOUT CREATING your personalized Emergency Emotional Support Plan (EESP). The strategies you learned in your anxiety and flourish type chapter, along with the mindfulness practices and the "what not to do" tips, are all *preventative* practices. They are the daily or weekly things you'll do consistently to refill your emotional bank account and prevent yourself from getting too depleted. The purpose of your EESP, however, is to arm you with strategies to use when you need in-the-moment support. Whereas the flourish strategies are like taking vitamins every day or wearing deodorant, your EESP is more like chicken soup and Advil or taking a shower after you've stepped barefoot in dog poop. These are the tools you'll look to when you get into a fight with your best friend, learn about a school shooting, or find out you might get laid off. Don't worry, creating your EESP is quite simple—just read, have a pen in hand, and be honest with yourself. Nobody's watching. (OK, maybe somebody's watching, but they're not gonna care. In fact, they'll appreciate that you have a plan in place for when the shit hits the fan.)

Now that you know your primary (and probably secondary) anxiety style, understand the difference between true and surface self-care, and know your SuperSense, you have the foundation to create a powerful EESP. I've separated the strategies into three categories: 1-minute strategies, 10-minute strategies, and 30-minute strategies. Your job, *should you choose to accept it*, is to scan through these lists and **circle two or**

three strategies in each of the categories. This, my friend, will serve as your personalized EESP. I recommend ripping out these pages to post on your bathroom mirror, writing them down in your journal, and taking pictures of them with your phone and keeping them in "favorites." If your motivational style includes an accountability partner, share the pages with your trusted friend. Then buy them a copy of this book so they can learn about their anxiety style and create their own EESP.

"To know thyself is the beginning of wisdom."
— Socrates

1-Minute (or Less) Strategies

Take five slow, deep breaths. Slow, deep breathing will help to neutralize the sudden spike in cortisol and adrenaline surging through your system and reset your central nervous system. With each breath, try to exhale just forcefully enough to make a candle flame flicker but not enough to extinguish it. Close your eyes to reduce the stimulation in your visual cortex. Relax your shoulders and the muscles around your mouth and jaw. Then take five slow, deep breaths and just notice the sensations in your body.

Do a 30-second energy blast. This can work especially well if you've been sitting for a few hours staring at a computer screen. Stand up, go outside if possible, and move your body in a way that feels good. You can try doing 25 jumping jacks or find a nearby staircase and run up and down it three times.

Drink a full glass of water. So often, we are simply dehydrated. We've eaten, enjoyed our coffee, maybe even had some sweets. But we haven't had nearly enough water. For years I regularly carried Advil and Excedrin pills in my pockets because my headaches were so frequent. I later realized they were caused by dehydration. *Hangry* is the term folks often use when describing angry moods caused by hunger. Maybe we should coin a term for irritable moods caused by thirst: *thirritable*. Don't let yourself get *thirritable*. Drink more water. Bonus tip: add some trace minerals or squeeze some fresh lemon juice into it.

Practice an emotional boundary mantra. Say three times in a row, "My emotional health is just as important as the happiness of others," or "I am responsible only for my own emotional well-being," or "I can only control my own beliefs, words, actions." Smiling and breathing deeply while you say these mantras will help you recenter and unfluster yourself.

Pose in a power position. Stand up with your hands on your hips, feet spread apart, and chin tilted upward, and smile for 30 seconds. Breathe. Our brain takes notes from our bodies so that it can regulate our hormones and neurochemicals appropriately. If we're standing as if we feel confident and proud, our brain will begin to release the corresponding neurochemical recipe for confidence and pride.

Say a self-kindness mantra. "I give myself permission to accept how I feel fully," or "I am worthy, I am loved, I am safe," or "I am connected to the highest level of wisdom and light." Mantras are simple, free, and easy ways to brainwash yourself with positive, healthy messages. We spend much of our lives judging ourselves and speaking harshly in our inner dialog. It's time to counter those years of negative words with purposefully positive self-messaging.

Do one sun salutation. Moving through a yoga sun salutation is a simple and powerful way to ground yourself, move your body, and oxygenate the blood throughout your body. Take off your shoes and socks, feel your feet on the ground, and move through an entire sun salutation without any devices on or even within reach. Bonus points if you go outside and do it in the fresh air.

Chew gum. Chewing gum reduces overactivity in your central nervous system because your Neanderthal brain believes you must be safe from predators if you're eating. Your body is no longer preparing itself for battle. Instead, blood can flow back from your extremities to your internal organs. Your heart rate can slow down. Your blood pressure can fall. I keep a bag of pür gum in my work bag and on my desk, and dip into it almost obsessively. I've probably gone through 22 packs of it while writing this book.

Watch the clouds. Spend 30 seconds observing nature. You can watch the clouds move slowly across the sky, or watch a single branch move in the breeze. You can find a tiny bug on the sidewalk and watch it intently. Tuning in to nature can help to reset your central nervous system, ground you, and return your focus to the present moment. When you are safely in the present moment, it's much more difficult to feel flustered about the past or worried about the future. In the moment, we are almost always safe.

Feel free to add your own 30-second strategies below:

_____

_____

_____

_____

_____

10-Minute Strategies

Listen to a special playlist of songs. Sit in your car and listen to music you loved as a teenager. Your brain is particularly neuroplastic during your teenage years. This means that the music you listened to regularly and the movies you enjoyed at that age are ingrained in you more deeply and hold even more emotional meaning than recent music or movies. Have you ever raved about an old movie that a friend had never seen and then excitedly showed it to them, waiting for them to fall in love with it like you did? What happened? Were they like, "Um, yeah that was good, I guess." Unless they happen to be between 14 and 24 years old, you might not get a very big reaction from them. You can use this phenomenon to your advantage. Make a few different playlists of songs you loved during your teenage years. Then when you need a 10-minute mood boost, turn up the volume and enjoy.

Take a 10-minute stretching break. Remove yourself from whatever space you've been in most of the day; get out of the car, leave your office, or walk out your front door. Then put your phone on "do not disturb" and move your body in a way that feels good to you. Stretch. Twist. Lie down on the ground and put your feet up a nearby wall. Try to make your body as long as possible. Then gently fold in on yourself. Stay in each stretch only as long as it feels good. Remember to breathe deeply and slowly as you're moving. Try to remain mindful. Notice how your feet feel on the ground, on the wall, or in your shoes. Ten minutes of present-focused movement can do wonders for your mind and your body.

Reach out to a friend. Send a text or voice message to a supportive friend and say, "I'm not OK." Think of one or two people right now (who are *not* vampires, by the way) you trust to be supportive and kind when you reach out to them.

Friend #1: _____

Friend #2: _____

Great! These are the people you will connect with when you need emotional support. Be clear from the start of the conversation about what you need most from them: a safe place to vent for 10 minutes, their opinion regarding a challenge you're facing, or maybe a distraction because you've been spiraling. In that case, ask them to share what's been going on in their life lately.

Write in your gratitude journal. Remember the 20/80 journal from chapter 9? Spend 10 minutes in a quiet spot and journal your thoughts. I recommend you spend 20 percent of the page venting your feelings, no matter how extreme or overboard they might seem. Then spend the remaining 80 percent of the page on what you want. Write out what you want to have, be, do, or believe instead of whatever frustration or pain is happening in your life at the moment.

Listen to a 10-minute guided meditation. Our thoughts are powerful. Changing negative thoughts can feel like moving a two-ton boulder uphill in roller skates. Sometimes we need help—we need an outside guide, an expert. This is where guided meditations become a brilliant option. If you don't already have a favorite meditation app or meditation guide, reach out to your woo-woo friends and get their recommendations. I love Emily

Fletcher's and Gabby Bernstein's meditations. Throw in your earbuds, sit comfortably, and just listen. When you get distracted (or you distract yourself), just circle back and refocus your attention on the meditation.

Take your coffee on a walk. If it's feasible, I recommend you take your coffee on a walk around the block, without your phone. I swear, it's possible to leave your phone somewhere for 10 minutes. Everyone will survive. (I cannot guarantee it, but it's highly likely.) Breathe. Move your body. Walking with both of your arms swinging is the ultimate cross-lateral movement. These movements encourage the electrical currents in your brain to function in a more cohesive way. Then just look around. Observe. Notice the subtlest sound you can hear, the slightest scent you can detect, or the smallest bug you can see flitting around.

Take an afternoon mindfulness shower. During quarantine home-schooling, this became one of my go-to mental health strategies. In the afternoon, when I began to feel my patience wearing thin and my eyes glazing over, I got naked. Well, I locked myself in the bathroom first. Then I got naked and hopped into a toasty shower. Try it yourself one afternoon. Make sure your phone is either in another room or silenced. (Notice a pattern with the phone component of these strategies?) Once you're under the showerhead, use a mindfulness technique to slow your brain and breathing. You can repeat a simple positive mantra like, "I'm so grateful my loved ones are safe, happy, healthy, and together." Try to zone out and watch the drips of water on the tile wall beside you. You can also close your eyes and tune in to the subtlest sound you can hear. I often find that 10 minutes in an afternoon shower (I don't even wash my hair) leaves me happier, nicer, and far less flustered for the next several hours.

Throw yourself a solo dance party. This strategy counts for exercise too, so it's doubly awesome. I close my bathroom door, search "old school hip-hop" on YouTube, and let the music take me. I pretend I'm 22 and in a club—except it's so much better because (1) I'm not trying to dance in heels, (2) nobody's trying to hit on me, (3) I won't have a hangover the next day, and (4) it doesn't reek of smoke. (Yes, millennial moms, people used to be able to smoke in clubs. Can you believe it?)

Have a laugh fest. Having a belly laugh releases natural endorphins to help you feel more joyful and less flustered. Find your favorite comedian, sitcom, or blooper reel online. I highly recommend the "Friends Bloopers Gag Reel Season 1–10" on YouTube. I've probably watched the entire thing seven times, and it's over an hour long. Give yourself 10 minutes of laughing so hard that tears are streaming down your face. It's a complete physiological reset. You'll feel like an entirely new human when you're done.

Do a guided qigong breathing practice. This breathing practice is often utilized to reduce stress, inflammation, and blood pressure. If you're new to it, I recommend going to a class or attending a workshop with an expert first. People have varied responses to this practice—from deep, emotional, cathartic release to relaxation to the point of instigating a deep sleep. (Yes, this is the same breathing practice I mentioned in the Fighter mom exercises.)

Linger on the best-case scenario. Visualization is a positive and powerful way to ease your fluster and calm your nervous system. As a protective momma, you likely imagine worst-case scenarios all the time. I get it. That's why it's important to purposely challenge yourself to instead imagine the *best*-case scenario. Get into the details and feel the feelings if at all possible. In my book *Stretch Marks*, I share my G.O.O.D.I.E. visualization practice. It combines all my favorite components of the most powerful visualization tools into one practice.

Take a silly afternoon playtime break. As adults, we rarely take time to do anything creative just for the sake of fun. I recommend you step into the uncomfortable zone, as my friend Missy, CEO of CatTongue Grips, says. Get silly. Make a fool of yourself in a physical way. Do any physical activity you wouldn't typically do, like hula hooping, roller skating, or jumping on your kid's trampoline. Skip down the street like you're in third grade again, or grab some chalk and draw out a hopscotch game on the sidewalk in front of your apartment. This is a great option when you need a lift while you're in charge of the kiddos. When your kids have the opportunity to see you as playful and silly, they'll connect with you on a whole different level. A playful afternoon break with the kids can bring you closer together and put everyone in a better mood for the remainder of the day.

Feel free to add your own 10-minute strategies below:

_____

_____

_____

_____

_____

30-Minute Strategies

The following list of strategies are powerful, because you'll chose one that is emotionally replenishing for *you*. I recommend selecting an activity that was either helpful to you in the past or is something you've secretly (or not so secretly) wanted to do for a long time. Remember, these 30-minute strategies are not fluff. They're not treats or rewards. These emotional support strategies are just as important to your emotional well-being as healthy food is to your physical well-being. If you're emotionally over-whelmed and don't take the time and energy to effectively address your emotional state, it can affect your work, physical health, parenting, sleep, and relationships.

- Go to your favorite yoga or Pilates class.
- Find a quiet place and meditate.
- Draw, color, or craft without your phone or computer nearby.
- Bake or cook your favorite meal.
- Learn a new hobby. (Try something you've always wanted to learn, like guitar, salsa dancing, or Italian.)
- Read in a quiet room with a cozy blanket.
- Take a coffee break with a friend at your favorite coffee shop.

- Schedule three activities in the next month that will bring you joy.
- Take a hot bath with Epsom salts and light a lavender-scented candle.
- Work on that book project you've been thinking about for the last six years.
- Go on a walk, hike, or run in a place that brings you joy.
- Make a phone date with a dear friend who makes you laugh.

Feel free to add your own 30-minute strategies below:

- _____
- _____
- _____
- _____
- _____

Implementing Your EESP

Now, this is important: Remember those strategies you just circled in each category? Those are now your EESP. However, just knowing what tools you have at your disposal is only 20 percent of the solution. You have to actually *use* them when you need them.

We're now going to shift our focus to that remaining 80 percent: implementation. Let's make it as easy and simple as possible. Following are three ways to make it more likely you'll get yourself the help you need, when you actually need it most. How does that sound?

Keep Your EESP Where You Can See It

Type it up, take a picture of it with your phone, or write it out on a big blank piece of printer paper. Better yet, do all three. Post your EESP on the inside of your bathroom door. Keep a copy in your car. Write out your EESP on a small piece of paper and fold it up inside your wallet. E-mail yourself a copy and mark it as a "favorite" so you can find it easily. Also, put it in the "notes" section of your phone. Get the picture? You want to be able to access this really, really easily. I want you also to accidentally see your EESP at least once a week. The more often you see it, the more likely you'll be to ask yourself, *Could I benefit from any of these strategies right now?*

Tune In to Your Triggers

Look back at the common triggers you identified in the last chapter. The more self-aware you are, the more quickly you can process and then restore yourself to a healthy emotional state. Now this doesn't mean you ignore your feelings or skip over real human emotional responses. If you just lost a grandparent, yes, grieve. Take care of yourself and give yourself the time and space and grace to feel all of it. The EESP will help later, when you need to come up for air and get back into your life again. The triggers I'm talking about here are mostly the tender spots, the areas where your emotional response is acute either because your emotional bank account is low or because your anxiety style has left you with some sensitivities in this area.

Share It with Your Supporters

Remember the vampires? OK, let's see, what are the opposite of vampires? EMTs, maybe? Yeah, that works. If you are fortunate enough to have people in your life who are there when you need them and can help resuscitate you, share your EESP with them. Your EMTs are people you trust, who know you well, and who want to see you happy and healthy. They are not competitive with you or jealous of you, nor do they judge you in any way. EMTs have your back. Always. If you have someone like that in your life, first, be very grateful. Send them a text right now and tell them how much you appreciate them in your life. Second, make sure you show up for them in the same way they show up for you. Third, share with them what you've learned in this book thus far. The next time you're feeling low, are flustered, or are completely losing your mind, give them full permission to ask you, "Have you tried one of your EESP strategies yet?"

Spread the Joy

Positive vibes are contagious. Good self-care is contagious. Self-compassion is contagious. You can be that epicenter of good for your family and your friends. If you think more moms deserve to flourish, each time you implement one of these strategies, share what you've done for yourself online with the hashtag #unflusteredmom (unless it's an unplugged strategy; in that case wait until you've finished!). Each time you hear of someone taking the time to do something for their mental and emotional health, you are far more likely to do it for yourself. Be that spark for those around you. Sometimes, they are just waiting to give themselves permission. You can be a positive example. Not only will it help other moms, but their responses will make it more likely that you'll continue your self-care practices. For instance, you can post "I just took a walk by myself! #unflusteredmom" or "I just took a guitar lesson! #unflusteredmom" or "I'm taking the night off guilt-free! #unflusteredmom."

Sleep

Any book, workshop, or course that teaches emotional resilience and well-being cannot overlook the impact of sleep. And nobody knows sleep deprivation like mothers know it. Nobody endures months and years of interrupted and insufficient sleep like someone raising children. I remember feeling so frustrated about not sleeping well during my first pregnancy. Everyone told me to sleep now, because once the baby arrived, I wouldn't get to sleep. So much pressure. But I was so huge and uncomfortable, I just couldn't sleep—which, in turn, made me anxious about not sleeping well, which then made it harder to sleep well. A vicious circle. Then a friend of mine dropped a simple, yet depressing truth bomb that stopped that circle: "Stop trying to sleep well now. It's too late, and you're not going to sleep well for the next 18 years." There was something freeing in that message, whether it was true or not. I could relax my unrealistic expectations about how I should or shouldn't be sleeping as a mother-to-be.

As luck would have it, I didn't have to wait 18 years to sleep well again. It only took 11. I'd graduated from Tylenol PM to Lunesta to Ambien and still wasn't sleeping well. I'd crash out at 11:00 PM only to find myself wide awake three hours later, my mind racing and my body somehow wide awake. Once I learned transcendental meditation, all of that changed. And it changed fast. If you're intrigued, grab Emily Fletcher's book *Stress Less, Accomplish More* or take one of her courses. The magic is simple, yet powerful, and so incredibly worth it.

Here's the thing about sleep: Many moms don't sleep well, regardless of their kids' ages, regardless of the amount of stress in their lives, regardless of their marital status. And many of the moms I work with have long since given up on the prospect of ever sleeping well again.

Here's why I cannot let you give up: (1) there is hope, and (2) the costs of not sleeping well are too big. Lack of sleep affects your body, mind, soul, and relationships. Even poor-quality sleep leads to an early decline in memory and cognitive functioning. Remember that "mommy brain" bullshit? Well, I say put anyone through the kind of sleep deprivation torture that most mothers endure and tell me if they can possibly think straight.

Lack of sleep and poor-quality sleep contribute to fertility challenges, cardiovascular disease, chronic inflammation, car accidents, immune system dysfunction, and depression. Bad sleep affects mood, concentration, focus, and problem-solving skills. The following sections detail my top tips for better sleep. Try just one of these for the next week. If all goes well, add another the following week. And so on. Then please shoot me an e-mail at hello@ambertrueblood.com to let me know how well you're sleeping. My assistant Gerusa created a beautiful pdf of sleep tips for you to download at www.ambertrueblood.com/downloads.

Tip #1: Keep It Steady

Go to bed and wake up about the same time every single day. Even weekends. Many sleep researchers agree that regularity of sleep and wake times affects how easily you fall asleep and how well you stay asleep each night.

Tip #2: Keep It Cool

Try dropping the temperature in your bedroom by two degrees. Our bodies are more likely to stay asleep if we're cool than if we're hot. Try opening a window or turning on a fan as well.

Tip #3: Keep It Dark

Your circadian rhythms are strongly affected by light. On your phone and computer, use an app like Redshift that adjusts the brightness and color temperature of your screen according to the time of day—this will help tell your brain to wind down for the night. Also, if the sun rises earlier than you do, use curtains or wear an eye mask to ensure light doesn't interrupt your sleep. When we were traveling regularly, we kept blue painter's tape and giant black trash bags in our suitcases. We'd cover the bedroom windows with the trash bags when we stayed in a hotel or an Airbnb without dark curtains or blinds.

"Routinely sleeping less than six or seven hours a night demolishes your immune system, more than doubling your risk of cancer."
—Matthew Walker, professor of neuroscience and psychology at the University of California, Berkeley

---

Tip #4: Keep It Quiet

Pull out that baby white noise machine or download a white noise app on your phone (then put the phone in airplane mode, of course). Use earplugs and a white noise app if you live in a particularly loud area or have cawing birds waking you up at 4:00 AM. *Don't they know it's not dawn yet?* If your SuperSense is auditory, this one is particularly important for you.

Tip #5: Keep It Clear

Many people are sensitive to electricity or Wi-Fi signals. Yeah, it's probably not great for any of us to be surrounded by these 24/7, but for some the effects are magnified. If you have a router (you may need to sit down for this one), turn it off at night. *What? Are you crazy?* Listen, I've been doing this for over a decade and I assure you it's not only possible, it's also freeing. Several members of my family sleep better without Wi-Fi running throughout the house. Also, I recommend unplugging anything plugged into the wall where your bed sits. Plug it in elsewhere in the room if you can. If it's a lamp or a clock, use a battery-powered option or just pull out the plug before you go to bed. Try it for a week and see if you sleep better or notice any other shifts in your body (like fewer headaches, for instance).

Tip #6: Keep It Calm

Spend the last 15 minutes before bed doing some sort of physically calming practice. Take a bath, do a gentle stretch, try a deep breathing exercise, or walk on the grass outside to ground yourself.

"It is disquieting to learn that vehicular accidents caused by drowsy driving exceed those caused by alcohol and drugs combined."
—Matthew Walker

Tip #7: Keep It Moving

Sleep researchers agree that people who exercise during the day sleep better at night. When your body is confused, it won't sleep. If it's unsure if it's day or night because of artificial light, it won't sleep well. Similarly, if you've been stationary all day long, your body doesn't understand that now is time to rest because it's been kind of been "resting" all day long.

Tip #8: Keep It Sober

I know, I know. I didn't like this one at first either. But, as I got older, I could no longer ignore it. The effects of drinking alcohol became even more obvious. Now, if I drink a glass of wine late at night or have two margaritas at dinner, holy cow do I sleep awfully. Drinking alcohol or using THC to sleep is merely sedating your body. As soon as the sedative effects wear off, your body wakes up (even if it's 3:00 AM). Do not confuse sedation with sleep. Your brain doesn't. The replenishing and restorative qualities of REM don't happen as easily under sedation. Your body needs nondrugged sleep to maximize your mental faculties and to truly physically rest.

Tip #9: Keep It Sleep-Only

Your body takes cues from its surroundings all day, every day. It learns your route to work, so that you can zone out and think about other things and still manage to drive to the right place. It begins to salivate around dinnertime and feel anxious every time you walk past that pile of bills on the table. If you watch TV in your bedroom, work on your presentation in your bedroom, or do workouts in your bedroom, your brain and body might be confused. *Am I supposed to give you a burst of energy? Do you need to focus and concentrate? Or, are you trying to sleep now?* Reserve your bedroom for resting and sleeping (and making out with your partner). Eventually, your brain will learn to wind down every night when you step into your bedroom and begin your bedtime routine.

---

*"When sleep is abundant, minds flourish.
When it is deficient, they don't."*
—Matthew Walker

What You've Learned About Creating Your EESP

- Tune in to your top three trigger signs.
- Keep your EESP close at hand.
- Share it with your EMTs.
- To sleep well, keep it *steady, cool, dark, quiet, clear, calm, moving, sober, and sleep-only.*

My EESP: The Worksheet

You can also find, download, and print out EESP worksheets at www .ambertrueblood.com/downloads.

My Common Trigger Signs:

_____

_____

_____

_____

_____

1-Minute Self-Care Strategies:

_____

_____

_____

_____

10-Minute Self-Care Strategies:

_____

_____

_____

_____

30-Minute Self-Care Strategies:

_____

_____

_____

_____

11

TALKING WITH WORDS

AT ONE POINT WHEN OUR BOYS WERE LITTLE, I remember my husband saying he felt like he was living with a drill sergeant. Yes, he meant me. I was a stay-at-home mom with four little ones, three of whom were still pooping in diapers at the time. When he called me a drill sergeant, I wanted to rage like a 1970s cartoon character with smoke billowing out both ears. But, I also felt deeply flustered and embarrassed. Because . . . he wasn't exactly *wrong*.

All the vulnerability and softness in my personality had vanished. The lighthearted, easygoing version of myself had been replaced with a serious, structured, grouchy, opinionated, bossy, demanding dictator. It was true. I didn't know how to be any other way at the time. I didn't know how else I could possibly survive that period of motherhood. I felt so anxious and flustered. How could I possibly maintain those soft, light, funny, sweet moments when I was perpetually exhausted, flustered, and worried about everything and everyone? How could I be sweet and easygoing while simultaneously trying to keep everyone safe and alive hour by hour? We both loved our boys so much and appreciated our new, bustling family. But I was in over my head. I was internally panicking, constantly treading water with my head just barely above the surface. I felt like if I stopped moving, I might drown. Jaimie didn't know what to say or how to help me. He felt like he didn't even know this person I'd morphed into.

The drill sergeant comment could have marked the start of a bitter feud between us. Instead, it created an opportunity for me to share honestly and vulnerably with him just how very awful I felt. I didn't want to be some militaristic, bitter robot, but I didn't know what else to do. The bossiness was my attempt at feeling a smidgeon of control amid all the chaos. The structure was my way of trying to fit a *Titanic*'s worth of chores and responsibilities into the space of a canoe. The grouchiness was just a result of my total physical exhaustion. Now I realize that anyone who's woken up four times a night for five years would be equally low on patience, compassion, empathy, flexibility, or playfulness. At the time though, I felt guilty that I'd created all these little lives and couldn't handle them with ease and grace.

The point is this: I was totally a drill sergeant because I didn't know how to be any other way. It was my survival technique, good, bad, or ugly. It seemed to work too. Except that I felt awful about it, and it pushed Jaimie and me apart. Gone was the woman he'd met and married. I'm sure it scared the shit out of him. Communicating more directly and more honestly, in a respectful and compassionate way, is what saved us. Saved me. Saved our family. When he learned and understood how scared and exhausted I felt, he was able to show more compassion. When I told him what I needed more of, he was able to step up and act in a way that truly helped me. And, when he saw more glimpses of original-recipe Amber, things really started to shift for us. We reconnected. We became a team. We felt gratitude and respect for each other instead of frustration or disappointment.

We also, as mentioned in my first book, *Stretch Marks*, were both only children raised by single moms. Together, between the four of our biological parents, we experienced nine divorces. Yes, *nine*. So we came into our relationship with a deep understanding of how fragile a marriage can be and how easily it can either fall apart or explode in flames. This kind of respect for our relationship put us in a unique position. We didn't want to wait and hope things would magically "get better" or "work themselves out." Instead, we were highly motivated to figure out how to communicate and resolve our issues as quickly and fully as possible.

The Return on Investment

After reading this far into the book, you understand yourself and your anxiety patterns a little bit better. You know your flourish type and can acknowledge and celebrate it. You know your triggers and your Super-Sense. You have true self-care strategies and mindfulness practices to fill up your emotional bank account. And you have a customized plan with strategies to reduce your fluster and overwhelm in a way that works best for you. Fantastic! Now, let's take it a step further. As mothers, much of our stress and anxiety stem from our relationship—or get dumped into our relationship. When your relationship is going well, the support, acknowledgment, and security you feel can help lighten the emotional load of the rest of your life. But when things are not going well, it can feel like you're trying to run a marathon, in the dark, alone. In a storm. In flip-flops.

This chapter gives you tools to reduce the amount of stress and frustration coming from your relationship. It'll also help you become more cognizant of dumping on your partner when you're flustered in other areas of your life. By learning and implementing these simple communication strategies, you can reduce the load of anxiety and stress you're carrying—and get more of what you want in your relationship. You're going to learn how to communicate so that you feel more supported, more acknowledged, and more appreciated by those who matter most. Imagine a large ship barreling across the ocean into a storm. There are bright, sunny skies just off to the left, but you're heading straight into a mass of dark, swirly clouds. One tiny shift of the wheel (rudder?) can turn the entire ship just a few degrees. In almost no time at all, you're in sunny skies again. The seas are calm. You're back in control. You feel happy and confident and secure.

Healthy communication in your relationship works the same way. It's not complicated. But chances are you've been using less-than-ideal methods of communicating your needs and your flusters to your partner. With the simple tactics in this chapter, you can shift your entire relationship. It doesn't take a lot of work or energy, but it *does* take action. It does take making a clear decision that it's worth it to you. It also takes vulnerability, honesty, patience, and humility. I'm confident you can do it.

I often say to my clients, "It may not be easy, but it's almost always very simple." One or two tiny, itsy-bitsy turns of the wheel can have a tremendously positive impact on your relationship (and on your family). Many of the communication strategies we're going to discuss in this chapter are practices you might already know how to do. But, because you're overwhelmed, resentful, or exhausted, you're just not doing them right now. Or, you might learn a strategy you have never heard of. Either way, it's OK. Let's dig in, shall we?

Anxiety and Your Relationship

When our relationships aren't going well, a lot suffers—our health, our work, the emotional health of our children, and more. Relationship miscommunication and conflict is a big part of overwhelm and stress for moms. Your fluster levels rise when you're arguing with your ex about spring break schedule, fighting with your partner about money concerns, or resentful about the lack of support and appreciation you feel every day. Depending on your particular anxiety style, you will get different benefits from utilizing these communication strategies. Focus on the benefits that are most important to *you*. When you think about all the positive changes that can happen when you level up your communication skills, you're far more likely to actually implement the strategies on a regular basis.

♥ When Lover moms feel emotionally disconnected from their partner, they can feel *hurt*. They might think "If they really loved me, they would do *this*, say *that*, etc." It can feel personal and painful when Lovers are not emotionally intimate with their loved ones. Once you invest your time and attention into shifting your communication style just a little bit, you can feel more deeply aligned with your partner.

● When Visionary moms feel emotionally disconnected from their partner, they can feel *frustrated*. The feeling is often based on the perception "If they understood what I'm trying to do, they would say this, do this, say that, etc." It can be annoying to take the time or energy to explain what you need and want from your loved ones. Once you utilize your new communication tactics, you'll be far more likely to get the support and encouragement you want and deserve.

★ When Dynamo moms feel emotionally disconnected from their partner, they can feel *disrespected*. The feeling is based on the perception "If they respected me, they'd know what to do and to say." A Dynamo can feel sad and unworthy when they're not emotionally connected with their loved ones. Once you implement your new communication strategies, you can get consideration and acknowledgment you desire.

■ When Executive moms feel emotionally disconnected from their partner, they feel *uncertain*. The feeling is based on the perception "If I'm not feeling connected with and supported by my partner, maybe I'm not safe." It can seem uncomfortable and unstable when Executives are not emotionally connected with their loved ones. Once you create a new way of communicating with your partner, you can depend on your partner more easily and more often.

▲ When Fighter moms feel emotionally disconnected from their partner, they feel *alone*. The feeling is based on the perception "If we don't connect, it just reminds me that I am on my own in this life and I can only rely on myself." It can seem like a familiar disappointment when Fighters are not emotionally connected to their loved ones. When you learn to communicate more effectively with your partner, you'll allow your partner to step in to save and support you more often.

How to Get More of What You Need

Step #1: Get Honest

If you have a history of handling a majority of the household responsibilities, your partner may not fully realize the emotional toll it's taking. As the daily tasks of motherhood grow, most moms just keep taking on more and more and more until their health suffers, their marriage suffers, or they find themselves popping open the pinot noir at noon. I recommend expressing yourself clearly and calmly when the workload becomes too much to handle. Start simple. Don't wait for your partner to figure it out on their own. You might assume that your overwhelm is obvious, and then feel hurt and resentful when your partner doesn't step up to offer their help or support. Waiting silently or even giving hints won't get you the result you need, want, or deserve. Again, do not wait for your partner to figure it out on their own.

"Don't make your community and loved ones guess what you need. It's not fair to them. Instead, proactively tell them—in an uplifting way—how to love you."
—Lisa Nichols

Instead, I want you to get honest. Be crystal clear about your current mental or emotional state. For instance, you can say, "I'm at a breaking point right now." Or, "I've hit a wall." Or, "I am not OK." Choose a phrase you have not said a million times before (like "I'm exhausted"). In fact, quantifying your level of emotional and physical energy may be a helpful way to communicate how "done" you are.

Brené Brown often shares her personal relationship strategies. For example, if she's had a rough day, she tells her husband where she is on a scale of 0 to 50. Zero means completely bankrupt in her emotional bank account, and 50 means she feels great emotionally, physically, and mentally. Her husband also shares his number on the same scale. The goal is to make sure that the numbers equal at least 100. If one partner's is lower than 50 and the other has extra in his or her emotional bank account, that partner can step up. However, if their numbers combined don't equal 100, then they need to either let something go or get outside help. For instance, if one partner is at 40 and the other is at 60, that's fabulous. If they're both at 40, then they're short and need to cancel the weekend plans and make frozen pizza for dinner.

> *Ask yourself: Where is my emotional bank account today on a scale of 0 to 50? If I'm not at 50, what can I let go of? (Maybe the laundry.) What true self-care can I add? (Try a nap.) How can I ask for the help I need?*

Step #2: Actions Speak Louder than Words

If you tell your partner you need a break, make sure your actions match your words. Many partners will take notice of your actions more often than your words. Say something new and match it to your actions when you say it. For instance, sit down. (Or lie down.) Don't say, "I am not OK" while you're running around still doing everything. Matching your actions to your words will give you a much better chance that your partner will hear your words. Most men tend to be more visual than auditory. For most women, the opposite is true. Men, then, will pay more attention to what you *do* than what you *say*. For instance, if you say "I'm so happy," but you lie in bed and cry all afternoon, your husband will get nervous and worried. If you say "I'm really unhappy," but you make a healthy dinner, smile, and read bedtime stories to the kids, he'll likely come to the conclusion that you are totally fine. Unfortunately, most women do the latter. Be careful that your actions are not overriding your words. If your partner isn't getting the message, ask yourself, *Are my actions sabotaging what I'm trying to communicate to my partner?*

💜 🟦 This strategy can be particularly powerful for Lover and Executive moms.

> Ask yourself: Do my actions match my words today?

Step #3: Share What You've Done

Getting honest with your partner and sharing your current state of mind is only the first step. It's extremely helpful (to you) if you also share what you've already done. Moms often assume that our partners already know all the responsibilities we're juggling. (Psst: they don't.) Chances are you've become so adept at completing so many tasks that even *you* don't realize all you've accomplished in a given day. I recommend occasionally posting a "public list" in your home where you detail the upcoming 20 to 30 items you're working on. Then, as the days go by, cross them off as you complete them, but leave the entire list on display. Next, be really honest with yourself about which of those tasks you (1) enjoy doing, (2) don't enjoy doing, (3) don't enjoy doing but really don't want anyone else to do, or (4) don't mind doing but would really love some acknowledgment and appreciation for it.

For the tasks you enjoy doing, make sure nobody takes them from you thinking they're helping. For instance, my husband offered to read bedtime stories to the boys one evening because I was really tired. I said, "No thanks, that's one of my favorite bonding times with them. But it would be awesome if you would finish cleaning up the kitchen." For the tasks that you don't enjoy doing (and are happy to delegate), ask for specific help with those. Let your partner know directly that although you *typically* do them, you really don't like them. (Note: Many men will make the assumption that if you keep folding and putting away everyone's clothes, you must enjoy it.) Feel free to correct that assumption in all applicable cases. For instance, "I know I normally fold all the laundry, but I really hate doing it. Would you do the folding tonight while I finish these e-mails?" Next, for the tasks you don't mind doing (but would love acknowledgment for your efforts), express that by saying something like, "Ugh, pulling together all our tax paperwork is so tedious and stressful. I might need a neck massage later tonight!"

Note: Before you ask for specific help, it's useful to express what you've already chosen to delegate, delete, or delay for another time. For instance, you can say something like, "I decided to push back everyone's dentist's appointments until after the holiday break because there's just too much going on right now. And I asked my mom to help with taking the boys to their soccer games this weekend since you'll be out of town. But I still have a lot of work to do for our tax paperwork." *Then* ask for the specific help you need from your partner. "So can you pick up the kids from school tomorrow and take them to a park and then to dinner? If you all stay out until after seven, I can probably finish all the forms. That would be so helpful."

If your partner asks why you have to do the forms now when they're not due for a few more weeks, do yourself a favor and take the time to explain why. What, in your opinion, is the unwanted consequence, potential danger, or emotional toll that will result if you don't do it now? After a few times explaining your thinking, it's likely your partner will begin to assume you have a dang good reason for whatever it is you're trying to do now. You won't have to explain your thinking for the next 40 years. Take a deep breath and, in a totally non-snarky tone, take the time to explain your reasoning.

■ ▲ This strategy can be particularly powerful for Executive and Fighter moms.

Step #4: Ask for Something Specific

Let's dig in a bit deeper on asking for what you want. Instead of voicing what isn't working for you, focus on what you do want. Many moms hope (or hint) at what they need more of in their relationship. And when that need isn't met, hurt feelings and frustration often abound. Unfortunately, setting up your partner for failure doesn't benefit anyone. Instead, directly say what you want and make sure you're kind, specific, *and* mention the benefits. For instance, "Could you finish cleaning up the kitchen tonight while I finish editing these articles? Then we'll be done at the same time and can watch a movie together!" Or, "Tomorrow when you get home from work, can you take the kids to the skate park for two hours so I can take a shower and record these videos?"

Imagine you're driving a car. Your entire family is in the car. You're singing to the baby so she can fall asleep, helping your fifth grader with his math homework, trying to follow the GPS, handing out healthy snacks to everyone, and you really have to pee, but you're running late. Not safe, right? Then it starts to rain, and the kids are fighting and you're about to lose your mind. You very briefly consider driving into a wall. This is when I want you to pull over, stop the car, and get out. Ask yourself this question: *What is most important to me in this moment?* (In this metaphor, it's finding a restroom and getting the kids a snack.) Maybe the math homework can wait. Or maybe Dad can drive while you sit in the back to get the baby to sleep, or Dad can talk math with little David. Get your own priorities straight—not what you think you *should* do, but what you actually feel is most important at the moment. Then get really specific in expressing what you need and want more of.

▲ This strategy is fantastic for Fighter moms.

> *Ask yourself: Have I asked for*
> *exactly what I need today?*

Let's Review
- **Step 1: Get honest.** Say, "Honey, I have too much on my plate right now and I can't handle it all."
- **Step 2: Match your actions.** Make sure your behavior matches your words. Ask yourself, *If someone only saw my actions today, would they know what I'm trying to communicate?*
- **Step 3: Share what you've already done.** Tell your partner what you already let go of, put off to another time, or delegated to someone else. For instance, "I asked my mom to come this weekend, I pulled out leftovers for dinner, and I'm gonna leave that laundry for tomorrow."
- **Step 4: Make a specific ask.** Ask your partner to do something very specific and tell them how it benefits you (and them). "Can you take out the trash cans before dinner and pick up takeout so that I can take a walk and calm my brain down? That would be really helpful and make me so happy."

Why Doing Less Is OK

Here's an annoying truth: Sometimes the person you're upset with is right. Don't hate me! Your partner might say, "Why do you keep volunteering at the school if you're so overwhelmed?" Listen, just because it's annoying to hear doesn't mean it isn't a valid point. If the same question came from a girlfriend, your therapist, or that old lady at church who's always telling inappropriate jokes, would you consider it seriously? Maybe you have a dang good reason for volunteering at the school, like you really enjoy it and it's the highlight of your week. Or there's a potential bullying situation going on and you're trying to get some perspective on what's really happening. Or, *maybe he's right*. Maybe you don't love it, you don't "need" to be there, and it's draining your limited time and energy. Sometimes it's helpful to take a moment and consider whether you're killing yourself unnecessarily.

> ## Ask yourself: What can I let go of today?

Feeling worthy of a break, help, or support is a huge part of the battle for many moms. Intellectually, we know we need and deserve a break. But somehow, for some reason, we still feel guilty for even *wanting* a break. Like needing a break from your family or mom responsibilities somehow means you don't like, love, or appreciate being a mom. Not the case at all, right? Let's look at it from another perspective. Do you know of any jobs where you're on the job seven days a week, night and day; you don't get paid any cash money; you don't get vacation time; you cannot take sick days; and you have to clean up both poop and vomit on a regular basis?

Even if you love absolutely everything about being a parent, it's a lot. You love your children. You love being a mom. You feel so grateful for your family. I get it. And, you still need a break. Let me repeat this. **You still need a break.** You deserve it. Everyone in your family will benefit when you take breaks more often. Wanting and needing (and dreaming about) a break doesn't mean that you are not grateful for your family. If you absolutely love key lime pie, you wouldn't necessarily want to eat it seven days a week. You might need a break from it. If you love watching old episodes of *Friends*, you still might want to throw in an episode of *Succession*. If you love taking hot baths, you eventually need to get out and grab a sandwich. I heard someone quoted saying he's tired of having sex with a Victoria's Secret model. Everyone needs a break, regardless of how good they may have it. Parenting is the same. Taking a break is not only reasonable, it also will benefit your emotional health, your parenting patience levels, and your relationship with your partner tenfold.

You might find that you love and enjoy your parenting role even more after you've taken the time to give yourself a break. Unfortunately, when you're a mom, the love and connection and enjoyment of parenting is entangled with the responsibility and pressures and chores and worries. It's the constant work of being responsible for another human being. A break from that responsibility—an evening, a day, a weekend of being responsible *only* for yourself—can be the greatest central nervous system reset for a mother. You can rest, relax, and refuel yourself. You can be off-duty biochemically and physiologically. Even if and when you do take a break, it can be hard to turn it off, right? Have you planned a getaway but prepped all the meals beforehand, called from your destination to make sure the kids don't forget their soccer cleats, and then texted to remind them about the piano lesson at 6:00 PM instead of 5:00 PM this week?

One of my podcast guests, entrepreneur mom Renée Warren, recommends taking Tuesday Nights Off. Every Tuesday night, she's off-duty from 4:00 PM on. She can use that time to meet girlfriends for dinner, watch Netflix in bed, do a yoga class, take an online workshop, and so on. It's nonnegotiable. If the kids have soccer or a playdate or a doctor's appointment that evening, her husband is responsible for it. She said that, at first, she'd switch around the night, depending on that week's schedule, so she'd be home on nights that were busy. Renée soon realized that this was unfair to herself and unnecessary. Now, it's a regular part of their family schedule. Mom gets Tuesday Nights Off.

As a working-from-home mom and homeschooling mom in a home with five men, I recently spent three nights in Palm Springs with a couple of girlfriends. Now I make a point to do it once a quarter. I often meet my mom and sister there for those three days. During those three days, I am responsible only for myself. My sister brings the food, I schedule the Airbnb, and my mom takes care of the wine. We talk, read, eat, drink, and soak in the hot tub. I work too, because I love what I do. The last time I went, I spent the first night alone and did zero work. I watched a Netflix comedy show, ate fish and chips from a delivery service, drank Nigori sake, then had an early dance party by myself in the living room before calling the boys to read *Harry Potter and the Goblet of Fire* on FaceTime and going to sleep by 10:30 PM. It was marvelously refueling for my body, mind, and soul. Everyone in my home experienced a much happier, more patient mama when I returned.

Let's normalize mom breaks, shall we? Can we all agree that our families are better off with happier moms? Can we all agree that moms need breaks? Can we all agree that moms deserve breaks? Can we all agree that when moms take breaks it benefits almost everyone around us? Can we all agree that guilt doesn't do us any good? Can we all agree that glorifying the exhausted, self-sacrificing mom isn't serving us any more? (Not that it ever did.) Let's begin a new trend. Normalizing mom breaks. Modeling healthy self-care. Glorifying self-compassion. Can we be kinder to ourselves and show others that it's actually our responsibility to take care of our emotional well-being? Let's make self-compassion go viral. Can you imagine?

"My mission in life is not merely to survive,
but to thrive; and to do so with some passion,
some compassion, some humor, and some style."
—Maya Angelou

What If You're on the Brink of Divorce?

What if you're already so disconnected from your partner that you're not sure the relationship will survive? Maybe you're not sure you want it to survive at this point. Many couples tend to have circular arguments. They fight about the same topics over and over and over again. Nothing seems to get resolved. Instead, life gets busy and things feel OK for a bit. A few months pass. Then the shit hits the fan all over again and you're arguing about the same thing, except now you're even more agitated and flustered because you keep trying to make your point and your partner is just not understanding, respecting, or listening to you!

The following five strategies are powerful tools for navigating a relationship that's been struggling for a long time.

Approaching a Tricky Conversation

Broach the subject only after both of you have eaten, slept well, and, ideally, not had too stressful of a day.

Start by expressing *your feelings* instead of focusing on your partner's words or actions.

Ideally, start the conversation outside on a walk or during physical activity *without* your devices in hand. This is not a conversation to start at the end of a long day, in your bedroom, or on your way to a family get-together.

Before starting the conversation, remind yourself of your ideal outcome. What are you hoping for? What do you want most for your relationship? How do you want to feel more connected and aligned?

Sharing your answers to these questions is a fantastic way to begin the conversation as well!

Take Your Argument for a Walk

If you hold in your frustrations all day and then blurt out everything you've pent up at bedtime (and in the bedroom no less), it's a surefire way to start a big, juicy argument. When either partner is hungry, tired, stressed, or distracted, trying to discuss something difficult might leave you both feeling emotionally disconnected and incredibly frustrated. At that point, it's unlikely either of you will feel heard, supported, respected, and loved. The fresh air, physical movement, and lack of distractions will help you feel more emotionally connected, heard, and understood.

⬤ ▲ This is a great strategy for Visionary and Fighter moms.

Say One Thing

Most of us crave more compliments, words of appreciation, acknowledgments, or apologies. Who doesn't love feeling seen and valued by those we love? Choose one of these categories and make a point to relay it to your partner every day for a week. Chances are, when you apologize to or compliment your partner more often, your partner will begin to reciprocate the behavior. It's human nature. Don't believe me? Try it! Creating a spiral of good, positive interactions is far healthier than maintaining the status quo of cutting complaints or snarky comments.

★ This is a great strategy for Dynamo moms or anyone feeling underappreciated.

Take Space, But Use Your Words

Sometimes your level of frustration is so high that you can hardly stand being in the same room as your partner. Taking some physical space is important. However, explain clearly why you need the space and what you're hoping will come of it. For instance, "I'm feeling really frustrated and unappreciated right now. I'm going to go for a run after dinner so that I can clear my mind and not say or do something that'll just make it worse." Verbally explaining what you're doing can be extremely helpful for a partner who may easily jump to conclusions or assume the worst if you temporarily disappear (either emotionally or physically).

If your relationship has been struggling for a long time, or you've gone for years feeling disconnected, disrespected, and unappreciated, then your emotional bank account might be very, very low. Women tend to give and give until we hit empty. Unfortunately, even if you and your partner are still living together as a married couple, if you've hit zero in your emotional bank account, you might just be going through the motions, but your heart is done. You've given all you can give and have nothing left. If you're not quite down to zero yet, I urge you to read on and use that remaining balance to try something new.

💜 This can be tricky for a Lover mom, but if you can do it, it'll be really powerful.

Reconnecting with Your Partner Emotionally and Physically

According to Brené Brown, "Connection is the energy that is created between people when they feel seen, heard, and valued; when they can give and receive without judgment." When looking to reconnect with your partner, try the following steps:

Step 1: Every night for a week, write down three specific qualities you appreciate about your partner. We naturally focus on what isn't working well. Purposefully focusing our attention on the positives gives us a more accurate view of reality and makes for a far more pleasant relationship. Doing an appreciation practice right before bed will also reduce stress and anxiety in your life and increase the chances you'll wake up in a good mood. The more specific you can be, the better. Bonus points if you actually tell your partner what you listed or share your appreciation in a note at the end of the week!

▲ ✸ This can be particularly powerful for Fighter and Visionary moms.

Step 2: Tell your partner when you feel happy. We often walk around feeling stressed, distracted, or anxious—and it shows. Facial expressions, body language, and tone of voice communicate the worry or frustration we feel inside. It's likely your partner is worried about you and feels responsible for your emotional state. Sharing your happiness out loud (with eye contact and a smile) will remind your partner that it's not all bad and that they're (hopefully) not all to blame. This is an exceptionally powerful yet simple strategy to rebuild a close emotional connection with your partner. Many women, for instance, don't realize that the man in their life is pulling away (emotionally) because he feels like he's failing in his job to make you happy. Nothing he does works, so he pulls away. Show him he's wrong, and you just might be surprised to see how he lights up again. Any time you feel happy, look him in the eyes and say, "I'm so happy right now. This is fun."

♥ ▮ This strategy can be particularly powerful for Lover and Executive moms.

Step 3: Apologize. All humans appreciate a good, genuine apology once in a while. Imagine if someone you knew 20 years ago sent you an e-mail out of the blue to apologize for wronging you in some way. How would you feel? Imagine your partner apologized to you for something they said or the tone they used last week? How would you feel? Good, right? Giving genuine, heartfelt apologies when you've done or said something you regret will reconnect you more deeply with your partner. You'll also find that the vulnerability that comes with apologizing can increase the emotional connection in your relationship. Lastly, the practice of apologizing to your partner (or anyone you love) increases the chances that your partner will begin apologizing to you as well.

▲ ⬤ This can be particularly powerful for Fighter and Visionary moms.

Step 4: Say "You're right!" (when they're actually right). No matter how "wrong" your partner is on a daily basis, you can always find something they're right about. Give them props for being right, and it'll win you lots of relationship points. For bonus marks, say "you're right" in front of the neighbors or in front of your kids. Many of us are so hard on ourselves that we can really use a pat on the back from someone we care about. Hearing "You were totally right" from your spouse will send them the vital message: *I notice you. I see you. I value you.* Any time you can send someone you love these messages, it'll serve to strengthen the foundation of your relationship.

★ ▲ This can be particularly powerful for Dynamo and Fighter moms.

Step 5: (Bonus Step) Get a little bit naked. Skin-on-skin contact at bedtime often leads to more physical intimacy, which can help ease tension and facilitate a deeper emotional connection. The endorphins you release during a sexual encounter can help reduce stress and anxiety as well. I recommend changing up the clothes you sleep in or crawling back in bed with your partner (if you've been sleeping in another room) instead of *talking* about becoming more intimate. Actions speak louder than words, especially in the bedroom. For instance, if you normally sleep in full jammies, try wearing underwear and a tank top. If you normally sleep in underwear and a tank top, try just the underwear. If you normally sleep naked, try putting on a silky nightie. Then cuddle up to your partner and see what happens naturally.

♥ ■ This can be particularly powerful for Lover and Executive moms.

Moving Forward

If you're ready to hang up your drill sergeant uniform, you owe it to yourself to take action. Try something different. If you're waiting for the situation to magically improve on its own, you're doing the same things and expecting a new outcome. Remember the axiom: "Insanity is doing the same thing over and over again and expecting different results." I don't want you to have to wait one more second to start getting more of what you need and what you deserve in this life. I also want you to feel supported, acknowledged, valued, appreciated, and cared for. I want you to reconnect with your partner more often and more deeply before it's too late, before your emotional bank account hits zero.

I recommend you implement the tools in this chapter one by one. Start with the simplest strategy and apply it as genuinely and consistently as possible. Take your relationship in your hands right now. I have full confidence that you will begin to see the situation shift for the better. It may take some time—just as the disconnect likely took some time. But 99 percent of the time, it's worth the effort and you will be very glad you did it, not just for your partner or for your children's sake, but for *your* sake as well.

12

YOUR FLUSTER IS TOTALLY FLUSTERING MY FLUSTER!

NOW YOU KNOW YOUR OWN ANXIETY STYLE, understand your triggers, and have the skill set to manage your flusterment like a pro. If you're married or in a relationship, you might find that the last chapter was helpful, but perhaps too general. In this chapter, we'll get really specific about what happens when a mom with your anxiety style connects with someone of another type. If you're dating, you can have them take the quiz. If you're married or in a relationship, you probably already have a pretty good idea of what their anxiety style might be. If not, you can either scan the part II chapters and take a guess, or have them take the quiz at www.flourishquiz.com.

If you're not in a romantic relationship, you likely have another adult in your life you get to (or *have to*) interact with regularly. The quality of your adult relationships affects your children both because it affects you and because they watch it all unfold from their front-row seats. Perhaps your mother-in-law lives with you, or your ex has split custody and lives nearby. By understanding the opportunities and challenges between your anxiety style and theirs, you can vastly improve your relationship. In fact, I recommend you take a moment and look at the five interconnecting circles below. Write your name next to your dominant style. Then write the names of all the important adults in your life next to what you know or believe to be their primary style.

Now, as you scan through this chapter, read about the combinations that are most relevant to the important relationships in your life. You and your mother. You and your partner. You and your manager. You and your best friend. You and your father. You and your sister-in-law. You get the point. Perhaps you'll have an aha moment that allows you to release old pent-up frustration and resentment and forge a path to a new, positive, deeper connection with that person.

First, we'll talk about the five combinations that have the least in common with each other. When these combos show up in a relationship, the thing that will help you improve your relationship the most is *seeking to understand*. It's very difficult to muster compassion for someone's words, actions, or even beliefs when we cannot understand how they could possibly speak, act, or feel the way they do. Once we can understand others more deeply, we can release judgment, hold more compassion, and feel more patience. And when we bring more compassion and patience into our relationships, we often feel less resentment, frustration, aggravation, and hurt.

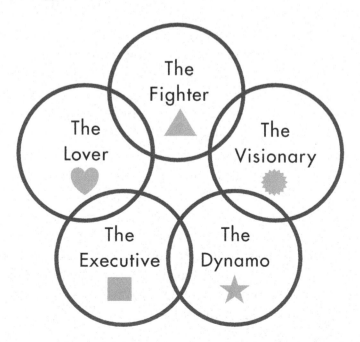

Write your name next to your dominant style. Write the names of all the important adults in your life next to what you know or believe to be their primary styles.

Complementary Styles: Seeking to Understand

Complementary styles are the nonadjacent anxiety styles on the model. These styles are more likely to have strengths that the other does not have. Like people, relationships vary tremendously. While some complementary partnerships may have a lot in common, others may have far less. The objective of this section is to identify and highlight where you align so that you may find gratitude and acknowledge what's working well in your relationship. Then, where you're not aligned, you can seek to understand so that you can feel more compassion and less aggravation.

The Fighter ▲ and the Dynamo ★

Where a Fighter leads with their gut, a Dynamo leads with their head. Fighters tend to focus their time and attention more on the present, while Dynamos tend to focus their time and attention on the future. While Fighters are often more extroverted and like to be around people, Dynamos are often introverts and feel refueled when they've had time to themselves. Fighters feel most alive when they are *being*, while Dynamos feel most alive when they are *doing*. When it comes to decision-making, Fighters may often make decisions based on their feelings, while Dynamos may make decisions after analyzing and thinking.

Luckily, this combo does share qualities as well, which is where they'll find connection and common ground. Both Fighters and Dynamos can deal well with the unknown, with chaos and change. They can both be dreamers and visionaries. And both thrive when dealing with challenges or emergencies. When the two of you are at odds, you can seek to understand your partner better by reminding yourself they might be focused on the present, while you're thinking about the future. Or, you might be basing your decisions on a gut feeling, while your partner is thinking and analyzing the decision.

Speak their language. If you know your partner is a Fighter, talk about your gut feelings and how something makes you feel instead of explaining your thought process or a bunch of facts and figures. If your partner is a Dynamo, talk more about goals and the tasks required to get to those joint goals. Ask them what they think about a situation instead of how they feel about it.

Find the common ground. If you know that you both work well under pressure and in emergency situations, reminisce about a time when you came together to help someone in need. Think of an experience where you were on the same page and felt connected to, and supported by, each other. This will increase the odds you'll better manage whatever current conflict you're having.

Remember the contributing factors. If your frustration and aggravation are creating a huge disconnect in your relationship, take a moment to remember (or find out) how your partner developed their anxiety style in the first place. If your partner is a Dynamo and you remember that their parents often linked love and attention to achievements, you might find more compassion for your partner when they feel constantly driven to do and do and then do even more. If your partner is a Fighter and you remember that they experienced severe bullying, not only in school but also from their father at home, you might better understand why they want to save and protect others from the same fate.

The Lover 💚 and the Visionary ⚫

Where a Lover leads with their heart, a Visionary tends to lead with their gut. Lovers typically focus their time and attention on the past and the present, while Visionaries focus their time and attention on the future. Lovers connect most with people and feel energized (or depleted) by their relationships, but Visionaries feel most fueled by spending time and energy on their dreams and ideas for the future. Often, Lovers find comfort in having control, knowing what to expect, and living in routine. Visionaries, on the other hand, thrive in an atmosphere of change, unknown factors, and unexpected challenges. Lovers are fabulous at *being* in the moment, and Visionaries are fabulous at *doing*.

One of the primary similarities between Lovers and Visionaries is how they approach decisions. Both tend to make decisions based on their feelings. They tune in to their intuition. When Lovers and Visionaries connect and form a relationship, it is often because what one is seeking (what is most difficult for that person) is exactly what the other is most naturally adept at. Visionaries should watch and learn how their Lover partner truly lives in and appreciates the present moment. The Visionary can learn from the Lover's ability to find joy in their relationships.

Our Lover mom Lisa was married to a Visionary. When her husband left the family, he said he felt held back by his responsibilities as a husband and father. He had a grand vision for his life, and it didn't appear to include Lisa. She was devastated and deeply hurt. Now, a decade later, his Visionary style doesn't trigger her as much as it did when they were married. He can now admire Lisa's ability to truly connect with their children and find joy and fun in the present moment. Lisa now understands that his leaving had little to do with his love for her and more to do with his single-focus approach to his dream of starting his own company. Surrounded by close friends and an amazing work team, Lisa no longer depends on her ex to feel worthy of love and attention.

Meet basic needs. If you know your partner is a Lover, slow down enough to make eye contact, touch them, ask a question about how they feel, and then just be still and listen. Listen without judgment, solutions, advice, or opinions. Spending at least a few minutes every day tuning in to your Lover partner in the present moment and being receptive to their needs will fill them up emotionally in a priceless way. If your partner is a Visionary, Lovers will benefit from very clearly expressing their needs and checking that their words match their actions. Remember, they are thinking in the future, focused on goals and dreams—and while it doesn't mean they don't love and value you immensely, they don't naturally know how to show it. Lover moms need to make it crystal clear how they need to feel supported and loved by their partner.

Find the common ground. If you know that you both function from feelings and intuition, use that to find a deeper level of connection. Often, remembering a time when you were on the same page and felt connected to and supported by each other will increase the odds you'll better manage whatever current conflict you're having.

Remember the contributing factors. If your frustration and aggravation are creating a huge disconnect in your relationship, take a moment to remember (or find out) how your partner developed their anxiety style in the first place. If your partner is a Lover and you remember that their mother was an alcoholic and their father left the family, you might find more compassion for your partner when they seem desperate for your acceptance, time, and attention. If your partner is a Visionary and you remember that they were deeply influenced by an uncle who started a huge company at an early age, you might find more compassion and understanding for their intense drive to accomplish such a big dream.

What can you learn from them? This partnership is special because the life lesson of a Visionary is well served by watching and learning from a Lover. A Visionary's primary lesson is to slow down and enjoy the people and the journey along the way to their life's mission. Lovers are particularly talented at being in the moment, connecting deeply with those they care about, and enjoying the good things in the present. This is a gift for Visionaries in relationships with Lovers. You have a wonderful example to follow.

The Executive ■ and the Fighter ▲

Where an Executive leads with their head, a Fighter leads with their gut. While Executives feel most comfortable and safe with routine and stability, Fighters feel most comfortable in chaos and change. Executives want to know the facts and what's going to happen so they can prepare and feel in control. Fighters are so accustomed to change that their worthiness is often intertwined with surviving challenges. When there are no challenges to survive, their identity can come into question and they can feel very uncomfortable.

Executives focus much of their time and attention on the future, while Fighters tend to focus on the past or the present. These two styles also tend to approach decision-making differently. While Executives research, plan, and analyze before making a decision, Fighters are more likely to tune in to their intuition. Lastly, while Executives feel most alive when they are *doing*, Fighters feel most alive when they are *being*.

Luckily, this combo shares one important quality, and this may be where you connect and find common ground. Both Executives and Fighters are more attuned to people and experiences than tasks or accomplishments. When the two of you are at odds, you can seek to understand each other better by reminding yourself that your partner might be focused on the present, while you're thinking about the future. Or, you might be basing your decisions on a gut feeling, while your partner is thinking and analyzing the decision.

Our Executive mom Elizabeth is married to a Fighter. Currently, it's not going well. She and her husband argue a lot, and she feels more disconnected than ever. Elizabeth holds the weight of responsibility of the household, finances, the kids, and holiday planning. The combative negative energy of her husband weighs her down emotionally, and she feels resentful. The couple does well when there's a family emergency, always coming together nicely in times of need. However, the rest of the time Elizabeth feels alone, exhausted, and angry. Here are some strategies Elizabeth can try:

Speak their language. If you know your partner is a Fighter, talk about your intuition and how something makes you feel instead of explaining your thought process or a bunch of facts and figures. If your partner is an Executive, give them the details and time to plan ahead so they can feel safe and prepared.

Find the common ground. If you know that you both value people and experiences most, reminisce about a time when you came together to help someone in need or had an incredible adventure together. Remember a time when you were on the same page and felt connected to, and supported by, each other. This will increase the odds you'll better manage whatever current conflict you're having.

Remember the contributing factors. If your frustration and aggravation are creating a huge disconnect in your relationship, take a moment to remember (or find out) how your partner developed their anxiety style in the first place. If your partner is an Executive and you remember that their childhood involved constant moving and starting new schools every few years, you might find more compassion for your partner when they feel the need to plan and schedule and control everything to the *n*th degree. If your partner is a Fighter and you remember that they experienced a lot of chaos and violence in their childhood, you might find more compassion when they seem to move toward conflict and chaos instead of away from it.

The Dynamo ★ and the Lover ♥

Where a Dynamo leads with their head, a Lover leads with their heart. Dynamos direct much of their time and attention on the future, while Lovers tend to focus on the past or the present. While Lovers feel most comfortable and safe with routine and stability, Dynamos find comfort in challenge and change. Lovers want to know the facts and what's going to happen so they can prepare and feel safe. Dynamos are content with chaos because it presents itself as a problem to resolve or a task to accomplish, which suits them nicely.

These two styles also tend to approach decision-making differently. While Dynamos research, plan, and analyze before making a decision, Lovers are more likely to tune in to their intuition and use their gut. And while Dynamos feel most alive when they are *doing*, Lovers feel most alive when they are *being*.

When the two of you are at odds, you can seek to understand the other better by reminding yourself that your partner might be focused on the present, while you're thinking about the future. Or, you might be basing your decisions on a gut feeling, while your partner is thinking and analyzing the decision. You might feel unsettled or flustered in the face of a big life change, while your partner might feel empowered and energized.

Speak their language. If you know your partner is a Lover, talk about your gut feelings and how something makes you feel instead of explaining your thought process or a bunch of facts and figures. Spend at least a few minutes every day tuning in to your Lover partner in the present moment and being receptive to their needs. This will fill them up emotionally in a priceless way. If your partner is a Dynamo, talk more about goals and the tasks required to get to those joint goals.

Ask them what they think about a situation instead of how they feel about it.

Find the common ground. Think of an experience you shared where you felt on the same page or had a common value. You can also think of a problem that you both get fired up about (from the same vantage point). Remember a time when you were on the same page and felt connected to, and supported by, each other. This increases the odds you'll better manage whatever current conflict you're having.

Remember the contributing factors. If your frustration and aggravation are creating a huge disconnect in your relationship, take a moment to remember (or find out) how your partner developed their anxiety style in the first place. If your partner is a Dynamo and you remember that their parents often linked love and attention to achievements, you might find more compassion for your partner when they seem constantly driven to do and do and then do even more. If your partner is a Lover and you remember that their mother was an alcoholic and their father left the family, you might find more compassion for your partner when they seem desperate for your acceptance, time, and attention.

The Visionary ● and the Executive ■

Where an Executive leads with their head, a Visionary leads with their gut. While Executives feel most comfortable and safe with routine and stability, Visionaries feel comfortable with chaos and change. Executives want to know the facts and want to know what's going to happen so they can prepare and feel in control. Visionaries tend not to be as sensitive to change or challenge. In fact, they may even feel energized and excited about it. While Executives focus on people and experiences, Visionaries are more attuned to accomplishments and are often comfortable alone.

These two styles also tend to approach decision-making differently. While Executives research, plan, and analyze before making a decision, Visionaries are more likely to tune in to their intuition.

Luckily, this combo does share important qualities as well, and this may be where you connect and find common ground. Both Executives and Visionaries are more attuned to the future than the past, or even the present moment. You also both tend to be *doers*. You are motivated, take action, and feel energized when in motion. When the two of you are at odds, you can seek to better understand your partner by reminding yourself that they might be thinking and analyzing (Executive) while you're tuning in to your intuition (Visionary). Or, you might be thriving during a chaotic situation (Visionary), while your partner feels flustered and anxious in the chaos (Executive).

Our Visionary mom Victoria shares a home with her Executive mother, Mirabelle. The two have a tricky relationship. Victoria appreciates her mother's help with the house and taking care of her little one so that she can follow her big dreams. However, her mother's constant need to plan and organize in detail is agonizing to Victoria. There's a lot of tension and frustration in the house, as they're still learning how to communicate with each other without resentment and hostility. They are using the following strategies to reconnect:

Speak their language. If you know your partner is a Visionary, talk about your intuition and how something makes you feel instead of explaining your thought process or a bunch of facts and figures. If your partner is an Executive, give them the details and time to plan ahead so they can feel safe and prepared.

Find the common ground. If you know that you both think about the future and are great at taking action, express your appreciation and gratitude for those traits. Remember a time when you were on the same page and felt connected to, and supported by, each other. This will increase the odds you'll better manage whatever current conflict you're having.

Remember the contributing factors. If your frustration and aggravation are creating a huge disconnect in your relationship, take a moment to remember (or find out) how your partner developed their anxiety style in the first place. If your partner is an Executive and you remember that their childhood involved constant moving and starting new schools every few years, you might find more compassion for your partner when they feel the need to plan and schedule and control their future. If your partner is a Visionary and you remember that they were deeply influenced by an uncle who started a huge company at an early age, you can find more compassion for their intense drive to accomplish such a big dream.

Sister Styles: Finding the Common Ground

Sister styles are adjacent anxiety styles in the model (see page 169). These styles are more similar to each other and can therefore find common ground more easily. Like people, relationships vary tremendously. While some sister-style partnerships might have a lot in common, others might have far less. The objective of this section is to identify and highlight where you align so that you can find gratitude and acknowledge what's working well in your relationship. Then, where you're not aligned, you can seek to understand and begin to truly feel compassion for each other.

The Fighter ▲ and the Lover ♥

Where a Lover leads with their heart, a Fighter leads with their gut. While Lovers feel most comfortable and safe with routine and stability, Fighters feel most comfortable in chaos and change. Lovers want to know the facts and want to know what's going to happen so they can prepare and feel safe. Fighters are so accustomed to change that their worthiness is often intertwined with surviving challenges. When there are no challenges to survive, their identity can come into question and a feeling of discomfort can abound. Lovers want to feel safe and connected, while Fighters are very comfortable under duress and even chaos.

Luckily, this combo does share several important qualities, and this may be where you connect and find common ground. Both Lovers and Fighters are more attuned to people and experiences than tasks or accomplishments. They're also both more likely to make decisions according to their feelings and intuition, instead of facts and analysis. In fact, Lovers and Fighters tend to feel most alive when they're *being*, not necessarily *doing*.

When Lovers and Fighters are at odds, it's likely related to their fundamental differences in where they thrive: Lovers flourish in safety and connection, and Fighters flourish in challenge and conflict. Our

Fighter mom Faith was married to a Lover. After many years together, they divorced amicably. They always respected each other's parenting style, honesty, kindness, and compassion. Unfortunately, they spent so many years focused on their children that they forgot to keep their relationship growing and connected romantically. They became just friends. Like roommates sharing children, they eventually agreed to lead separate lives.

Speak their language. If you know your partner is a Fighter, talk about your intuition and how something makes you feel. If you know your partner is a Lover, spend at least a few minutes every day tuning in to your partner in the present moment. Being receptive to their needs will fill them up emotionally in a priceless way.

Find the common ground. If you know that you both value people, experiences, and being in the moment, tune in to that. You both appreciate that special way of looking at the world. Remember a time when you were on the same page and felt connected to, and supported by, each other. This will increase the odds you'll better manage whatever current conflict you're having.

Remember the contributing factors. If your frustration and aggravation are creating a huge disconnect in your relationship, take a moment to remember (or find out) how your partner developed their anxiety style in the first place. If your partner is a Fighter and you remember that they experienced a lot of chaos and even violence in their childhood, you might find more compassion when they seem to move toward conflict instead of away from it. If your partner is a Lover and you remember that their mother was an alcoholic and their father left the family, you might find more compassion for your partner when they seem desperate for your acceptance, time, and attention.

The Lover 🖤 and the Executive ■

Where an Executive leads with their head, a Lover leads with their heart. Executives direct much of their time and attention on the future, while Lovers tend to focus on the past or the present. These two styles also tend to approach decision-making differently. While Executives research, plan, and analyze before making a decision, Lovers are more likely to tune in to their intuition to see how they feel about it. While Executives feel most alive when they are *doing*, Lovers feel most alive when they are *being*.

Luckily, this combo shares several important qualities, and this may be where they connect and find common ground. Both Executives and Lovers are more attuned to people and experiences than tasks or accomplishments. Safety feels like stability and control, knowing what will come and having time to prepare, if necessary. When the Lover and the Executive are at odds with each other, they can seek mutual understanding by appreciating the areas where their core values align.

Speak their language. If you know your partner is an Executive, give them the details and time to plan ahead so they can feel safe and prepared. If you know your partner is a Lover, talk about your intuition and how something makes you feel instead of explaining your thought process or sharing a bunch of facts and figures. Spending at least a few minutes every day tuning in to your Lover partner in the present moment and being receptive to their needs will fill them up emotionally in a priceless way.

Find the common ground. If you know that you both value safety and security, focus on that. Remember a time when you were on the same page and felt connected to, and supported by, each other. This will increase the odds you'll better manage whatever current conflict you're having.

Remember the contributing factors. If your frustration and aggravation are creating a huge disconnect in your relationship, take a moment to remember (or find out) how your partner developed their anxiety style in the first place. If your partner is a Lover and you remember that their father was an alcoholic and their mother left the family, you might find more compassion for your partner when they seem desperate for your acceptance, time, and attention. If your partner is an Executive and you remember that their childhood involved constant moving and starting new schools every few years, you might find more compassion for your partner when they feel the need to plan and schedule and control their future.

The Executive ■ and the Dynamo ★

While the Executive often thrives and feels most comfortable with people, the Dynamo is quite comfortable alone. Executives value safety and security, routine, and stability. However, Dynamos can feel energized when facing a challenge, changes, and even chaos, especially if it means they have a problem to solve.

Luckily, this combo shares many qualities, and these may be where you connect and find common ground. Both Executives and Dynamos lead most often with their head instead of their heart or gut. They both attend to the future more readily than the past or even the present. Both are *doers*. Executives and Dynamos tend to make decisions from a point of fact and analysis rather than intuition and feelings. When these two styles are at odds, both can seek understanding and find compassion by remembering their shared core values.

Speak their language. If you know your partner is an Executive, give them the details and time to plan ahead so they can feel safe and prepared. If your partner is a Dynamo, talk more about goals and the tasks required to achieve those goals. Ask them what they think about a situation, instead of how they feel about it.

Find the common ground. If you know that you both work well making plans and talking about the future, plan an event, experience, or vacation together that you both might enjoy.

Remember the contributing factors. If your frustration and aggravation are creating a huge disconnect in your relationship, take a moment to remember (or find out) how your partner developed their anxiety style in the first place. If your partner is an Executive and you remember that their childhood involved constant moving and starting new schools every few years, you might find more compassion for your partner when they feel the need to plan and schedule and control their future. If your partner is a Dynamo and you remember that their parents often linked love and attention to achievements, you might find more compassion for your partner when they seem constantly driven to do and do and then do even more.

The Dynamo ⭐ and the Visionary ●

Where a Dynamo leads with their head, a Visionary leads with their gut. While both are very goal oriented, a Dynamo might be more focused on the process (and enjoy the process) while the Visionary might be more focused on the final outcome. The Dynamo can feel adrenalized by the small achievements they accumulate over time. However, Visionaries might feel more easily frustrated by the process and the smaller, more tedious steps involved in achieving their dream. Dynamos also tend to make decisions from an analytical standpoint instead of an instinctive one, as Visionaries do.

Luckily, this combo also shares many important qualities, and this may be where they connect and find common ground. Both Dynamos and Visionaries are more attuned to the future than the past, or even the present moment. They both work well alone and are energized by their forward momentum and feelings of accomplishment. Dynamos and Visionaries tend to be doers. They are motivated, take action, and do well during times of change and conflict. When these two types are at odds, both can seek understanding and find compassion by remembering their shared core values.

Speak their language. If you know your partner is a Visionary, talk about your gut feelings and how something makes you feel instead of explaining your thought process or a bunch of facts and figures. If your partner is a Dynamo, talk more about goals and the tasks required to get to those joint goals. Ask your partner what they think about a situation instead of how they feel about it.

Find the common ground. If you know that you both think about the future and are great at taking action, express your appreciation and gratitude for those qualities in your partner. Remember a time when you were on the same page and felt connected to, and supported by, each other. This will increase the odds you'll better manage whatever current conflict you're having.

Remember the contributing factors. If your frustration and aggravation are creating a huge disconnect in your relationship, take a moment to remember (or find out) how your partner developed their anxiety style in the first place. If your partner is a Dynamo and you remember that their parents often linked love and attention to achievements, you might find more compassion for your partner when they seem constantly driven to do and do and then do even more. If your partner is a Visionary and you remember that they were deeply influenced by an uncle who started a huge company at an early age, you can find more compassion for their intense drive to accomplish such a big dream.

The Visionary ● and the Fighter ▲

Where Visionaries pay more attention to the future, Fighters tend to focus on the present and the past more often. Visionaries work well alone, so they can better focus on their accomplishments and dreams. However, Fighters tend to focus more on people and fairness, making sure to step in, fix, and save those who need their help. While Fighters feel most alive when *being*, Visionaries feel most alive when *doing*.

Luckily, this combo shares several important qualities, and this may be where you connect and find common ground. Both Visionaries and Fighters are comfortable with change, challenge, and even chaos. They're also both more likely to make decisions according to their feelings and intuition, instead of facts and analyses.

When the Visionaries and Fighters are at odds, it's likely related to the fundamental differences in where they flourish: Visionaries function primarily in a future-oriented state of mind while Fighters thrive in the moment.

Help each other. If you know your partner is a Fighter, help them to feel safe when all is calm and everyone is healthy and happy. Remember, they are reacclimating from an early life in high altitudes and low oxygen levels. (Skip back to chapter 8 if you have no idea what I'm talking about.) If you know your partner is a Visionary, help them to focus on present joyful moments as they make progress toward their big dreams. Encourage them to celebrate the little wins and smell the flowers along the way.

Find the common ground. If you know that you both value feelings and challenges, tune in to that. Remember and appreciate your special way of looking at the world. You can even decide to do a health challenge or a financial challenge together. Remember a time when you were on the same page and felt connected to, and supported by, each other. This will increase the odds you'll better manage whatever current conflict you're having.

Remember the contributing factors. If your frustration and aggravation are creating a huge disconnect in your relationship, take a moment to remember (or find out) how your partner developed their anxiety style in the first place. If your partner is a Fighter and you remember that they experienced a lot of chaos and violence in their childhood, you might find more compassion when they seem to move toward conflict instead of away from it. If your partner is a Visionary and you remember that they were deeply influenced by an aunt who started a huge company at an early age, you can find more compassion for their intense drive to accomplish such a big dream.

Identical Styles: Finding Balance

So you and your partner have the same primary anxiety style? It sounds like that would be ideal, right? I assure you it's not necessarily double rainbows and leaping unicorns. You probably find alignment and understanding more often than other couples do. However, you might also find that you amplify each other's fears and worries. Too much of the same sometimes leads to an imbalance. Also, like I mentioned at the start of this chapter, men often show they're flustered differently than women do. When you and your partner have identical styles, it's even more important to remember that while your partner might feel the same way as you, their signs and "symptoms" might look completely different. The objective of this section is to find where you're aligned and then recalibrate any imbalances resulting from being "too similar."

The Fighter Couple ▲

As two Fighters, you may approach the world differently, have very different personalities, and come from very different backgrounds. However, your core drivers are similar. You might find that you both lead from your gut and make decisions based on intuition and instinct. Now, you may not necessarily make the *same* decisions, but your process for making those decisions is similar. Utilizing language that expresses this shared approach can help when you're at odds. Phrases like "Something just feels off," or "That gave me goosebumps, I'm so excited!" will make sense to your partner (more so than to those with other primary styles).

While you both might feel comfortable amid change and conflict, you might also feel exhausted and drained. Years (or decades) spent in conflict, drama, protecting people, and standing up to the bullies of the world can take its toll. Physical ailments or emotional distress often show up in an attempt to get you to slow down and take a break. But that's not easy either, right? How do you feel when all is calm, when your job is going well, your health is good, your relationships are healthy? Do you feel uncomfortable? Off? Strange? Do you start to feel anxious, anticipating the inevitable moment when the shit will hit the fan all over again? Do you find it hard to enjoy the good stuff in life because you're accustomed to it slipping through your fingers just when you begin to feel happy? Do you rarely let your guard down because you've been taught (by life) time and again that it's just not safe to do so?

Maybe you and your partner both function in this capacity, drawn to and comfortable in chaos, but also exhausted from it. How do you start to slow down? How do you help each other notice and enjoy life more? How do you feel safe enough in your life to actually live? How do you embrace your superhero qualities as well as learn your life lesson—that you can be happy even without the drama and chaos? How do you create and acclimate to a life where you can rest, let down your guard, and allow more joy and light into your world? Using the preventative strategies in chapter 8 and your EESP from chapter 10 will help you get there.

Find courses, coaches, books, and friends that can help you become more conscious of the choices you make. Look at the areas of your life that feel chaotic and ask yourself, *Do I want more calm and ease in this area of my life? Do I kind of like that my relationship is dramatic, that I have huge financial wins and losses, or that my weight and health issues swing wildly? Am I tired of this? Am I ready for a new way of being? Do I want to allow more ease and joy into my daily life?* If your answer is yes, then together with your partner, look through the specific strategies in chapter 8. And revisit the communication strategies in chapter 11 that work particularly well for Fighters.

A Healthy Balance: Consciously decide where in your life you want challenge and where in your life you want ease.

I also highly recommend re-parenting practices like inner child meditations and writing letters to your parents about what you wish they had the capacity to do and say differently during your childhood. You can also talk to them about their childhoods to better understand what might have contributed to their parenting abilities (or disabilities). Maybe it wasn't your parents at all, but a bully in school, an abusive adult in your early life, or a traumatic physical injury. Please know that this work can be powerful. And powerful work often begins with darkness and pain before it gets to the light to find release. I highly recommend working with a trained mental health professional. You deserve to be a happy and healthy momma, and doing this work *alone* is not always safe, and it's definitely not ideal. Get real support before digging into any deep traumas. Find experts you can trust and lean on them as you heal your wounds. You are worth it, my friend.

The Lover Couple ♥

As two Lovers, you may approach the world differently, have very different personalities, and come from very different backgrounds. However, your core drivers are similar. You might find that you both lead from your heart and make decisions based on intuition and feelings. Now, you may not necessarily make the *same* decisions, but your process for making those decisions is similar. Using language that expresses this shared approach can help when you're at odds. Visceral phrases like "That makes me feel sick to my stomach" or "That gave me goosebumps, I'm so excited!" will make sense to your partner (more so than to those with other primary styles).

While you both might feel comfortable surrounded by friends and family members, you may be drawn to *different* groups of friends. You may enjoy *different* ways of connecting with people. It's well worth expressing to your Lover partner how you most love spending time with them. Do you love cooking with your partner, going for evening walks together, or talking on the phone during your lunch break? Spending quality time with your partner and getting individual attention fills you up on the inside. Find out what quality time actually looks like for your partner and do more of that.

What can be tough, though, is when work, friends, travel, or even technical difficulties separate you from those you care about. If it's anticipated and you can prepare for it, that can make it easier to stomach. However, if you don't know it's coming or there are last-minute changes, that can be hard. You both value feeling emotionally connected and spending lots of quality time enjoying each other. If both of you are fairly self-confident and self-aware, your shared Lover vibe can lead to a very intimate and especially fulfilling relationship. However, if there is significant distrust, insecurity, or emotional instability in your relationship, then conflict, jealousy, or misunderstandings can abound. When this happens in the life of a Lover, it's particularly brutal. Your relationships with your loved ones are everything to you. So when they're on shaky ground, or seem like they're already crumbling, it can feel like the worst possible experience.

If you feel disconnected from your partner, reread the strategies in chapter 11 that are particularly relevant to Lovers. It's also powerful to have the trigger talk described at the end of chapter 4 and to implement practices like the worthiness mantra and the nighttime tip jar to expand your sense of self-worth, inner confidence, and self-love.

Lover couples often focus a majority of their attention on the past (looking through old pictures and reminiscing about past adventures together) and the present (who is here with me right now). Unfortunately, this can sometimes lead to financial and health issues. Focusing on enjoyment in the present moment sometimes comes at the cost of future financial woes or health problems. They may get into financial trouble or find they've gained 40 pounds because they were so focused on enjoying the present moment.

> *A Healthy Balance: Enjoy and live your present life, without jeopardizing your future health or livelihood.*

Lovers can also become overly focused on meeting their partner's needs, so much so that they lose track of their own wants and desires. While it's admirable and beautiful to want to make your partner happy, you may regret doing it at the cost of your own identity or enjoyment. Again, it's about finding that healthy balance. How do you not become so intertwined that you can no longer separate your own needs and wants from your partner's? Lovers might also find themselves avoiding opportunities in their career or personal life that require a physical separation from their partner.

How can you find balance so that you can live and enjoy your life *and* have the connected, intimate relationship you desire? Continuing to build your self-worth so that more of it is based on internal factors instead of external factors will make a powerful difference. When you acknowledge, love, and attend to your emotional needs instead of depending on the words or actions of others to fill your bucket of self-worth, you've achieved your life lesson. When you learn to truly love yourself and acknowledge your own intrinsic value, you'll feel less triggered by the inevitable bumps and jumps in life *and* begin to flourish in many areas of your life.

The Executive Couple

As two Executives, you might approach the world differently, have very different personalities, and come from very different backgrounds. However, your core drivers are similar. You might find that you both lead from your head and make decisions based on research, planning, and organizing. Now, you might not necessarily make the *same* decisions, but your process for making those decisions is similar. Using language that expresses this shared approach can help when you're at odds. Using phrases like "I think that's a really good idea" will be more impactful than saying "I feel" or "I believe" to your partner. Sharing your thought process, the steps, and any supporting facts you've researched can also be helpful.

While you both might love being surrounded by friends and family members, you may be drawn to *different* groups of people. And you may enjoy *different* ways of connecting with those people. It's well worth expressing to your Executive partner what tasks and activities will make you feel more at ease and less flustered. As with any powerful communication strategy, being direct and specific (as long as you're respectful) is best. Maybe your partner feels frustrated and overwhelmed when the garage is a disaster and the household bills are disorganized. But maybe *your* Executive tendencies lean toward managing the kids' activities and schoolwork, and making sure there's always at least a half tank of gas in the car. Communicate clearly that your flusterment about a low gas tank feels the same to you as your partner's frustration with the bills. Relating your emotional status to a similar example of your partner's emotional status does two things: it shows them that you understand and see their frustration, and it allows them to better understand and respect your frustration.

What can be tough, though, is when big, unexpected life changes occur. Maybe one of you gets laid off from your job or transferred to a different region. Maybe one of your children moves out or gets married. Maybe a close family member becomes seriously ill. Maybe you get a big promotion that requires lots of last-minute travel. Maybe weather systems cause you to cancel your annual family vacation. Any big life changes, positive or negative, can undermine feelings of emotional well-being for an Executive. Knowing this, understanding yourself, and utilizing the tools in chapter 7 will help you feel safer, happier, and more connected to your partner.

If you feel disconnected from your Executive partner, circle back to the communication strategies in chapter 11 that are particularly relevant to Executives. Starting a hobby that safely gets you out of your comfort zone and avoiding zombies can support your emotional well-being.

Executive couples often focus a majority of their attention on the future. Unfortunately, this can sometimes lead to missing out on the present moment and having fun together. Couples with this style are often so engrossed in the state of *doing* that they refrain from *being*—even when it serves their best interests. When both parties are most comfortable *doing*, they don't slow down to enjoy the present moment and just *be*.

**A Healthy Balance: Plan and prepare enough
to feel safe and then take breaks, relax, and enjoy
the moment (and each other) more often.**

Executives can become overly focused on doing for the sake of doing without checking in with themselves to make sure it's actually important to them and worth their precious time, attention, and effort. While it's admirable and beautiful to work to keep everyone safe and everything organized, you may regret doing it at the cost of your own identity or dreams. Again, it's about finding a healthy balance. How do you create and protect your life *and* slow down and tune in enough to actually enjoy it?

Check in with yourself to ask, *What is the worst-case scenario here?* Then ask, *Can I handle that? What would I do if I ran out of gas on the side of the freeway on the way to my cousin's wedding with all the kids in the car? Could I handle that? What would I do if my kids missed soccer camp because I didn't remember to sign them up on time? Could I handle that? Could the kids?* Let's take it a step further and pose a third-level question: *What are all the good things that could come from running out of gas on the side of the freeway?* Maybe your children get to see Mom handle the situation well by calling AAA, texting family members so they won't worry, and playing a singing game in the car. Maybe that precious 45 minutes in the car with your kids ends up being a fun bonding experience and crazy story the kids will talk about for months afterward. Here are the three questions for checking in: (1) What's the worst that could happen in this specific flustering situation? (2) What would I do then? (3) What are all the possible good things that could come of it?

Granted, this may not work if your worst-case scenario goes straight to death or dismemberment. But, for all other potentially frustrating or challenging situations, it works very well.

The Dynamo Couple ★

As two Dynamos, you may approach the world differently, have very different personalities, and come from very different backgrounds. However, your core drivers are similar. You might find that you both lead from your head and make decisions based on research, planning, and organizing. Now, you may not necessarily make the *same* decisions, but your process for making those decisions is similar. Using language that expresses this shared approach can help when you're at odds. Using phrases such as "I think it's a good idea" will be more impactful than saying "I feel" or "I believe" to your partner. Sharing your thought process, including the steps and any supporting facts you've researched, can also be helpful.

While you both might be comfortable working and accomplishing alone, you might have different times of the day, week, or season when you can focus more easily. One of you may get your best work done early in the mornings, while the other is a night owl. It's well worth expressing to your Dynamo partner when and where you feel most productive. Then share specifically how your partner can support you in those projects and endeavors.

As with any powerful communication strategy, being direct and specific (as long as you're respectful) is best. Maybe your partner feels frustrated and overwhelmed when they're having technical difficulties and it's keeping them from accomplishing their goals. But, maybe your Dynamo tendencies become triggered when you spend much of your time and energy doing temporary-win tasks like preparing meals or cleaning the house. (By temporary-win, I mean tasks that don't feel like much of an accomplishment for a Dynamo.) Communicate clearly to your partner that your anxiety about the never-ending laundry is similar to theirs about the Wi-Fi signal interruptions, for example. Relating your emotional status to a similar example of your partner's does two things: it shows that you understand and see their frustration, and it allows them to better understand and respect your frustration.

What can be tough for Dynamos is when one partner feels the responsibility of the temporary-win tasks more deeply than the other. If that partner continues to push off their own personal achievement tasks, they can quickly feel flustered, resentful, and emotionally drained.

If this situation temporary, like when your partner is on a work trip, you can manage your emotional well-being by planning out specific times during the week (or after your partner returns) when you'll fully allow yourself to dig into your list and start accomplishing what truly invigorates and revitalizes you.

It boils down to self-awareness and communication. Know what feeds you and rejuvenates your spirit, and then find the time and space to do it consistently.

The more you do this, the more energy you'll create and the more patience and compassion you'll find for those you love.

Our Dynamo mom Daisy is married to a Dynamo. They both love achieving, planning, and setting goals. The couple managed to find different areas where each takes the lead. Daisy handles the finances and coordinates the household activities, while her Dynamo husband coaches the kids' soccer teams and plans the family camping trips. Both are working on slowing down and enjoying the wonderful life they've created. Ultimately, they've figured out how to support each other and make a good team both personally and professionally.

If you feel disconnected from your Dynamo partner, circle back to the communication strategies in chapter 11 that are particularly relevant to Dynamos. The "add a joy" and the shower mindfulness practices from chapter 6 will also deeply support your emotional well-being. Dynamo couples often focus a majority of their attention on the future. Unfortunately, this can sometimes lead to missing out on the present moment and having fun. Couples with this style are often so caught up in the state of *doing* that they refrain from *being*—even when it serves their best interests. When both parties are most comfortable *doing*, they don't slow down to enjoy the present moment and just *be*. It's about finding that healthy balance, where you're still getting that achievement high yet not missing out on the joys of your daily life.

How can you find balance so that you can live and enjoy your life *and* feel that energetic rush of accomplishment? Check in with yourself to ask: (1) What are the three most important things to me at this point in my life? and (2) Is what I'm stressing about right now (or trying to make time for) directly related to one of those three? If it's not related, then what can you do with this time instead that *is* related? Checking in and confirming alignment is a great tactic for Dynamos. It helps us from becoming so hooked on that adrenaline high that we spend a tremendous amount of time and effort on tasks that have nothing to do with what's most important to us.

Case in point: I once spent five and a half years going to night school to get a degree that I didn't need and didn't want, merely because I had made a commitment and was high on the roller coaster of accomplishing course after course after course. I wasn't even enjoying the classes! If I had checked in with myself, I would have realized that what I truly wanted was to be in a PhD-level clinical psychology program. Luckily, I eventually figured it out and began my psych program a few years later. I now have two MAs instead of one PhD, which, to be honest, still drives me nuts. I could have used all those years to get my PhD in a subject that truly lit me up. Lesson learned. As author Rebecca Campbell says, "Follow what lights you up, and you'll light up the world."

The Visionary Couple ❋

As two Visionaries, you may approach the world differently, have very different personalities, and come from very different backgrounds. However, your core drivers are similar. You might find that you both lead from your gut and make decisions based on intuition and feelings. Now, you may not necessarily make the *same* decisions, but your process for making those decisions is similar. Using language that expresses this shared approach can help when you're at odds. Using phrases like "Yes, that feels like the best option" will be more impactful than saying "I think" or "I know" to your partner.

While you both might be comfortable working and dreaming alone, you might have different times of the day, week, or season when you can focus more easily. One of you may feel very clear about your big purpose in this life, but the other might feel frustrated if they haven't yet figured out their purpose. It's important that Visionaries share what kind of support they need most right now. As with any powerful communication strategy, being direct and specific (as long as you're respectful) is best.

Maybe your partner feels frustrated and overwhelmed when the distractions of daily life are preventing them from making progress toward their goals. However, maybe your Visionary tendencies become triggered when you see that your partner knows exactly what they want to be doing, and you're not so clear. Communicate directly to your partner that your anxiety about not knowing your ultimate purpose is really bothering you. Maybe ask them how they felt before they fully understood their dream. Relating your emotional status to a similar example of theirs does two things: it shows your partner that you understand and see their frustration, and it allows them to better understand and respect your frustration. If you're a visionary waiting to uncover your dream, pay close attention to the story about ducks in the next chapter.

If you feel disconnected from your Visionary partner, circle back to the communication strategies in chapter 11 that are particularly relevant to Visionaries. The tiny moments and grounding practices from chapter 5 will also deeply support your emotional well-being. Visionary couples often focus a majority of their attention on the future. Unfortunately, this can sometimes lead to missing out on the present moment and having fun. Couples with this style are often so engrossed in the state of *doing* that they refrain from *being*—even when it serves their best interests. When both parties are most comfortable *doing*, they sometimes don't slow down to enjoy the present moment and just *be*. It's about finding that healthy balance, where you're enjoying and living your present life without jeopardizing future accomplishments or goals.

It can be tough for Visionaries to deal with tedious daily tasks like chores, meal preparation, school forms, social obligations, and small talk with strangers. Work together to figure out how to split up those unwanted but necessary tasks. What responsibilities can you delegate to your children? What tedious jobs don't have to be done at all (or at least not as often as others might do them)? What tasks can you pay someone else to do or trade services for? For instance, I have a dear friend who trades website design services for private yoga sessions. Think outside of the box, and you might surprise yourself with what is possible to take off your plate.

While Visionaries can become so focused on their grand plans, the non-Visionaries in their lives can often feel disconnected or even abandoned by them. Chances are you want and need your friends and loved ones in your life. Being purposeful about spending some of your time and attention on others can be very important for Visionaries. You don't want to find yourself at the end of your life having accomplished your dream with absolutely no one to celebrate with you.

> *Do not get so distracted by your life's purpose that those you love most in the world feel forgotten.*

How can you find balance so you can live and enjoy your life *and* reach your highest goals? Check in with yourself and ask: (1) Who is most important to me? (2) What do they need most from me? (Note: Check out their anxiety style to see what's most vital to them.) (3) How can I take time weekly to meet the emotional needs of those I love?

What You've Learned About Anxiety Styles in Relationships

- Couples in complementary-style relationships reconnect best by seeking to understand each other.
- Couples in sister-style relationships reconnect best by finding the common ground.
- Couples in identical-style relationships reconnect best by finding balance.
- Look at the preventative strategies in your partner's anxiety style chapter.
- Use the communication strategies from chapter 11 that work best for your particular style combination.

The Lover ♥	The Visionary ✹	The Dynamo ★	The Executive ■	The Fighter ▲

	Coming home to an empty house	Having nothing to accomplish today	Finding your fridge empty	Having lots of busy work
Excited/happy	✹	♥	▲	★
Calm/comfortable	★	■	★	■
Neutral	▲	▲	✹	♥
Uncomfortable/irritated	■	✹	♥	▲
Highly anxious	♥	★	■	✹

	A big health or $$ emergency	A big conflict with friend/partner	A long, lazy trip with friends	A big positive life change
Excited/happy	▲	▲	♥	▲
Calm/comfortable	★	✹	■	★
Neutral	✹	★	▲	✹
Uncomfortable/irritated	♥	■	★	♥
Highly anxious	■	♥	✹	■

FAREWELL TO FLUSTER

CONGRATULATIONS! BY TRULY UNDERSTANDING your anxiety style and implementing the tools most likely to support your emotional well-being, you've given yourself a tremendous gift. You now know that you are worthy of love, attention, respect, and acknowledgment. Even more important, you know that you are worthy of love, attention, respect, and acknowledgment from *yourself*. The funny thing is, when we truly feel worthy, we carry ourselves differently. We make different choices. We keep different company. We hold different expectations of ourselves and of those around us. We vibrate on a whole new frequency. We send a clear, energetic message to the world that we are, in fact, worthy.

It's totally human to want to also feel respected and loved by others. However, consider this when feeling hurt or disappointed as a result of others' actions or words: Who is this person? Do you share their core values? Do you respect how this person lives *their* life? How do they treat others? How do they show up in the world? For instance, we'd all love for our parents to be our biggest emotional supporters and cheer-leaders. It hurts when they don't have the interest or the capacity to show up for us consistently in a loving and supporting way. If you have a parent who *does* do this, fabulous. If that parent is still living, even more fantastic. But many of us have a parent who cuts us down, leaves us feeling unworthy, dumb, lazy, irresponsible, lost, or just plain wrong. If you can relate to this, be sure to ask yourself how much you'd value your parents' opinions of you if you were not related to them. Would you go the extra mile to seek their love and approval?

Feeling valued internally, intrinsically, from within—and by those *you* cherish and admire—that's the golden ticket. Often, your loved ones simply aren't capable of giving to you what they don't have themselves. (Read that again.) Perhaps they are still broken. And while it isn't your job to fix them, you can hold empathy for them. At the same time, you can feel worthy regardless of their capacity to express love and consideration. It's not about blame, it's about seeing them as the imperfect human they are. It's about understanding what they are and are not capable of. Trying to squeeze juice from a turnip is a terrible waste of your time and energy. My late mother-in-law Mikki used to say, "You can't change a tiger's stripes." Instead, let's focus on how *you* feel about *you*. That's where the heart of self-fulfillment lies. When you thrive in all the areas that are most important to you, you become unflusterable. When you are doing you, being you, showing up in support of the real you, you begin to truly flourish.

You can now move forward in your life by focusing your time, energy, resources, and attention on *what* is most important to you and *who* is most important to you. In the last two chapters, you learned communication strategies to get more of what you need and want in your life. More time to yourself. More help with the boring or hard parts of motherhood. More space to meet your needs. More connection and intimacy with your loved ones. More time with good friends. More reasons to treat yourself well and value your emotional health.

I recommend you regularly revisit the strategies and recommendations in chapter 11, because even though they work well, it's super easy to fall back into the communication ruts you've carved over the last couple of decades. And remember, it takes only one person in the relationship to change the way they communicate to spark a huge shift in the relationship itself. Be that change. Become the partner you wish you had. Focus on what is working well so that that amplifies. And get clarity about what isn't working well so you can communicate your needs differently from here on out. Remember, your loved ones really do want you to be happy; they often just don't know how to do it. Give them the gift of telling them what you need, showing them what you want, and raising your expectations of yourself at the same time.

By knowing your anxiety style triggers you can have more grace and compassion for yourself. With your newly evolved self-awareness, you can pour yourself a hefty helping of empathy for all your quirky imperfections. And once you connect the totally annoying and frustrating and sometimes infuriating qualities of friends and family (aka *their* "quirky imperfections") with their flourish type, you can more easily find compassion for them as well. When you better understand why your partner or your mother-in-law or your boss behaves a certain way, you can much more easily remove the "taking it personally" component. You can feel less triggered by their words or actions. You can respond less defensively. Perhaps you can even find some compassion for them. When you replace defensiveness or outrage with compassion, you respond differently to people. And when you energetically change the way you show up, they might begin to speak or even behave differently.

You've also learned in these pages that you, my friend, can flourish. Your flourish type laid the groundwork for you to develop incredible qualities, valuable skills, and special abilities that many people simply do not have. Acknowledging and appreciating your positive qualities not only will foster your self-worth and self-esteem, but also might deepen your compassion for people who don't naturally hold those qualities. When we feel frustrated with one of our children, for instance, it helps their development and future self-worth if we recognize that certain things may come easier for Mom than they do for a child or teenager. Helping your kids identify their own flourish-type powers can bolster their self-esteem and deepen the mother-child bond.

You now have tools and strategies you can use to reduce your daily stress and anxiety proactively. By implementing the weekly, daily, and multiday strategies of your primary and secondary anxiety styles, you can take control of your emotional state. You now hold the power to preventatively reduce the likelihood of feeling overwhelmed, regardless of the challenging situations that are bound to pop up in your life. And with your Emergency Emotional Support Plan at the ready, you've armed yourself with a customized toolbox of tactics to utilize in the moment, whenever you need them. Remember that the tools you circled in chapter 10 are your EESP. Choosing them ahead of time, before you actually need them, is the key to feeling less flustered. I recommend writing or typing out your top three 1-minute, 10-minute, and 30-minute strategies and e-mailing them to yourself with a subject line that's easily searchable, like "I Need Help Today" or "Crappy Day EESP Plan." Save your list in your phone notes. And print it out and post it behind your closet door or in a drawer, somewhere you will accidentally see it at least once a week. If you see it every day, it may soon become an invisible fixture that you don't even notice. Instead, place it where it'll surprise you about once a week.

Let's take a moment to review all five flourish type traits and life lessons before our precious time together comes to a close. As you read through these, think of a relationship in your life that's particularly challenging right now. Can you find (or admit to yourself) what *that person's* flourishing qualities might be? Can you spend some time ruminating on their gifts? Really dig in and call up example after example of something you truly respect or admire about them. We, as humans, spend an inordinate amount of time focused on what is wrong, what is not working. Our attention is drawn to what we dislike, what's irritating, what's harmful about someone else's behavior or choices. It's natural. This focus on the negative is very human. It keeps our species alive. However, it also keeps our species depressed, anxious, drinking, and flustered.

Some of us can more easily shift our focus to the positive and live in a state of gratitude more consistently. In fact, we all know someone who does this almost annoyingly well, right? Others have a much more difficult time focusing on the positive. These are often the folks who tend to think they're fooling or lying to themselves by focusing on the good. If *this* is you, I'd like to challenge you to consider this: What if your base assumption is incorrect? What if focusing on everything that could possibly go wrong actually doesn't protect you? What if it just makes you more miserable in the anticipation of possible, not probable, future disappointments? What if you could prepare (a bit) for the worst, and then focus most of your time, energy, and attention on what is working well in your life right now?

How the Lover Mom Flourishes

- ♥ You value your friendships and relationships greatly.
- ♥ You are generous with your time and attention.
- ♥ You are extremely observant of the needs and wants and moods of others.
- ♥ You are dependable and reliable.
- ♥ You are incredibly loyal, trustworthy, and conscientious.

As a Lover, you are driven by a deep desire to feel worthy of attention, affection, and love from others. But your work in this lifetime is to become the type of person who is worthy of attention, affection, and love from *yourself*. What are your personal core values? Who do you really want to be in this world? Imagine yourself at your 102nd birthday party, where your 99-year-old best friend is giving a speech about you. What would you want her to say? What type of life did you lead to make you feel so grateful, happy, and proud looking back over those 102 years?

All of the Lover recommended strategies are designed to support your life lesson. These practices help to remind you to acknowledge and appreciate the qualities you respect and admire most in yourself. The inner child work and meditations can allow you to more easily shift from self-worth based on the actions or words of others to self-worth based on you. By finding and growing the love within yourself, you can truly feel worthy and belonging always, no matter where you are or who you are with.

How the Visionary Mom Flourishes

- ● You can often see solutions to problems that few others can see.
- ● You can get fired up about a cause bigger than yourself.
- ● You can see the bigger picture more easily than most.
- ● You don't tend to get as distracted as other people do.
- ● You want to make a positive impact on this planet.

As a Visionary, you are driven by a desire to make an impact on the world. But your deeper work in this lifetime is to enjoy your life and the people in it as you journey toward your bigger passion and vision. You will still make an impact. It's just that your impact will be even sweeter if you smell the roses along the way. And step on the grass in your bare feet. And thank the gardener who planted those roses. And maybe cut one of them and give it to someone you love. Let's think about it this way: Sometimes you move so fast that the wake you leave behind could swallow up the people you care about most. You're like a tornado, with so much energy and momentum, but sometimes leave a trail of a mess behind you. Slow down to notice and appreciate the precious people and the special moments in your life. It will benefit not only those you love, but also you and your dream.

The recommended strategies for Visionary moms are designed to support your life lesson. These tools will help you notice and enjoy the tiny moments more consistently. The daily grounding practices will help you to be in the present moment more often and move your attention from your head back into your body. You may find that you feel less flustered when you spend more of your time and energy on slowing down a bit and engaging more deeply in the present moment. You may also find that the impact you wish to make in the world begins to flow more easily when you're not doing it completely alone, when you let people in, and when you calm your central nervous system.

How the Dynamo Mom Flourishes

★ You are more self-motivated and self-disciplined than most.
★ You can accomplish more in an hour than most people accomplish in a day.
★ You are energized by challenges that others view as daunting.
★ You are really good at planning and organizing.
★ You are a source of support and resilience for your friends and family.

As a Dynamo mom, you are driven by a desire to accomplish and earn the respect and acknowledgment of others. But your deeper work in this lifetime is to feel valuable and worthy of that respect and acknowledgment *regardless* of outside accolades. Don't worry. You can still accomplish a lot. You can enjoy it. I know you thrive in the getting-shit-done mode, and that is fantastic. However, you might find that by slowing down, by quieting your body and your mind, you become even more efficient and effective with your time. From that stillness comes insight and inspiration. From that quiet comes realization of your true core values. The more you can align that go-go-go nature of yours with what is truly important to you in this lifetime, the happier and more content you will be.

The recommended strategies for the Dynamo mom are designed to support your life lesson. These tools will help you slow down a bit and relish the wins more often. Practices like "add a joy" or open creative time can help you find fulfillment in the present moment more often. They will unlock the opportunity to connect more deeply with those you care about most. You may find that you feel less flustered when you take an afternoon mindfulness shower or outside nature walk. As a Dynamo mom myself, I still have to consciously remind myself to slow down, breathe deeply, and take breaks from my constant *doing* (and I flippin' wrote the book on this). It's a process. It's a balance. Be kind to yourself and, while accepting and staying true to your accomplishment-junkie nature, become purposeful in tuning into the present and connecting more deeply with those around you. Your work will benefit, your children will benefit, your relationships will benefit, and you will begin to flourish even more.

How the Executive Mom Flourishes

- You are always more prepared than others for unanticipated events.
- You are more organized than most people.
- You know where everything is, always.
- You are more dependable and responsible than most people you know.
- You can read people and situations really well.

As an Executive, you are driven by a desire to feel safe in this world by managing and controlling your surroundings and your future. But your deeper work in this lifetime is to feel emotionally safe regardless of what life throws at you. The world appreciates your organization, your planning, and your taking responsibility for so much. Maybe whatever environment or situation instigated this style for you isn't the case in your current life. Maybe you're in a safe home, safe community, safe job, and safe relationship. Maybe you can delegate some of your responsibilities more often. Perhaps you can let someone else take the reins for a bit, so that your constantly vigilant nervous system can take a break. Maybe you can choose one or two areas of your life that you don't control at all and see what happens. Letting go and realizing that you can handle whatever comes—that's the delicious lesson your heart can learn in this practice.

The recommended strategies for an Executive mom are designed to support your life lesson. These tools will help you to increase your emotional bank account and feel safe in your world, regardless of what may or may not happen in the future. Practices like avoiding zombies and neurohacks like the fake smile can help you boost your emotional reserves. New hobbies like roller skating or jujitsu can support your mental well-being as well as give you practice enjoying activities just for the sake it. Spend a bit more time in your day doing things that make you smile, make you feel connected with your family, and maybe even make a big fat mess all over the kitchen table. You can learn through these practices that not only are you safe, but also you deserve to enjoy the good things and good people in your life. Focus on the good at least as often as you worry about the potentially bad. I understand this may not be easy. As I often say to my clients, "It may not be easy. But it is often simple." Every time you worry about something that hasn't (and may not ever) happen, notice it. Then think of one thing that has happened and has had a positive impact on you, your family, your community, your pet, your finances, or your health.

How the Fighter Mom Flourishes

▲ You are a loyal and trustworthy friend.
▲ You go out of your way to help those in crisis.
▲ You feel energized when facing a challenge in your life.

▲ You are a survivor.
▲ You tend to be transparent, direct, and honest.

As a Fighter mom, you are driven by a desire to save and protect those around you. You are comfortable and at your best in the fight, in the scramble of life. But your deeper work in this lifetime is to shift from an identity based on *surviving* to one based on *thriving*. What if your deeper life lesson is to consciously decide when and where (in what areas of your life) you want to feel amped up by the challenge? Then you can begin to get more comfortable in ease, in safety, in healthy situations and environments. Your genius lies in that fighting spirit, and you get energized when the air is thin and you're again on top of the proverbial mountain. The magic happens when you become a conscious decider, choosing when you want to jump into the storm and save the day and when you want to sit back and be comfortable. When do you feel exhausted? When do you want to feel at ease in the calm, happy moments back on the beach amid a clear blue sky?

The recommended strategies for the Fighter mom are designed to support your life lesson. These tools will help you release the two-dimensional identity of the "survivor" and add a third dimension of "thriver." By regularly checking in with yourself, you can become more conscious of the choices you make in your career, finances, relationships, friendships, and parenting. You can decide how much drama and chaos you want in your life. Do you need a break? Has your system been working on survival mode for so long that it doesn't know how to rest? The qigong breathing practice can help you manually reset your central nervous system. Through the self-care strategies in your EESP, your mind and body can become more accustomed to calm over chaos. You can begin to enjoy feeling good and knowing you are safe in the world. You saved yourself, my friend. It is not your responsibility to now save everyone else. At least, not all the time. Deal?

Let's Do This

In this book, you've seen a lot of practical strategies: tools dependent on your motivational style, others influenced by your SuperSense, and, of course, tactics specifically tailored to your anxiety style. You've also created a list of your go-to strategies depending on how much time you have available to you at that moment: one minute, 10 minutes, or 30 minutes. You've learned communication strategies for your relationship, whether you're not getting your needs met, you want to reconnect more deeply with your partner, or you're on the brink of divorce and unsure of what to do next. All of those customized practical tools and recommendations don't have any value if they remain only in this book. Putting them into practice, one by one, *is the magic*. Understanding yourself and shifting your mindset is fantastic. It's a huge and necessary first step to getting you the life you want and deserve. But you cannot stop there.

Your life is too valuable, and you have too much good to spread in this world. Come back to this book regularly when you need it. Use your EESP when you need it. Start with the area of your life causing you the most stress right now and choose just one strategy to put into practice right away. Then keep at it. The issues you're struggling with didn't happen overnight, out of the blue. They've either been happening for a long, long time or they've been gestating for a long time. Either way, it will take determination and commitment on your part to change them. If that makes you sweat a little, revisit the motivation section in chapter 3. You can do this. You can. And it will be so worth it when you do.

Besides, your children deserve to have a mother who has her shit together and can then model and teach them these skills. Imagine how well they'll be able to handle ups and downs in their adult life if they have all the tools that you've learned here. Imagine the quality of their relationships if they know how to communicate their needs, manage their expectations, and more effectively navigate tricky conversations with emotional maturity and self-awareness. Imagine the quality of their physical health when they learn how to express their frustrations and flusters more effectively, sleep better, and get the support they need when they need it most. Imagine the quality of their financial life and career choices when they can manage their emotions better, minimize overstimulation of their central nervous system, and reduce feelings of overwhelm in a healthy way. Imagine how happy and confident they'll be when they've been taught self-awareness, self-worth, and self-understanding on a deep level.

Let's take a quick glance into the would-be future if you implement none of the strategies or tools in this book. What will your life look like in six months if you do nothing differently? How will your relationship look? What will your parenting look like? Will your patience levels be better or worse? How will your relationships look within your extended family? What will your friendships look like? How about work? What about your emotional well-being? What will your physical health look like? And, most important, how will you feel about yourself? Will you feel happy, safe, and proud of yourself? Will you feel truly worthy of joy, health, wealth, friendships, and love?

I want you to challenge yourself right here, right now. Commit to yourself that you deserve more. You deserve better. You deserve everything you want in this life. Sign below if you are ready to commit to yourself today that you are worthy of this work. You are worthy of a life of joy, health, wealth, friendships, and love.

> I, _____ hereby
> commit to myself, and only myself, that I am worthy of a
> flourishing life in every area that lights me up on the inside.
> I commit to myself that I will begin to notice my triggers,
> accept my imperfect self fully, celebrate where I flourish, and
> use the self-care tools I have learned here.
>
> Signature: _____
>
> Date: _____

I realize there will almost always be a reason not to start, not to forgive yourself, or not to move forward in the direction of your dreams. Author Mike Dooley tells a simple story about a momma duck and her baby ducklings. When the momma duck wants her ducklings to cross the field and go to the lake, she does not waddle around squawking at them until they line up neatly. Instead, she turns in the direction of the lake and starts waddling toward it. What happens then? Of course, the little ducklings quickly fall in line behind their mama and follow her. Life works this way too. If we wait until everything aligns before we begin walking, we will forever be waiting. There will always be a duckling out of line. Don't wait until soccer season ends before working on your marriage. Don't wait until your mom's hip surgery is over before improving your sleep. Don't wait until you lose 10 pounds before planning that trip to Florida with your best friend. Don't wait until you get that raise before you start a morning meditation practice. Almost all the strategies in this book do not cost any money, do not add any calories to your diet, and do not have negative side effects. None of them require you to have huge amounts of time or space in order to implement them into your life on a regular basis.

If you believe avoiding zombies or a mindfulness shower will help you feel happier, less stressed, and more connected to those you love, then do it. If you believe that listening to your favorite playlist or taking an unplugged walk around the block will help you regain your patience and calm more quickly, then do it. If you believe that matching your actions to your words will stop the fighting and bickering, then do it. Your life is in your hands. The choice is yours.

My Hopes for You

What I want for you most is to notice when you're triggered. I want you to implement the daily preventative strategies (from your anxiety style chapter) that most resonate with you. I want you to regularly use your EESP when challenges and setbacks inevitably pop up in your life. I want you to wildly celebrate your wins and achievements. I want you to consistently acknowledge your unique ways of flourishing. I want you to have grace with yourself. I want you to be kind to yourself. I want you to feel deep gratitude for what you've survived, what you've done, and what you've created so far in your life. When you come from a place of genuine gratitude, you open the floodgates to receiving more of what you want in this lifetime. I also want you to know you are worth it. You are worthy of it all. You can do, be, have, and give more than you ever thought possible.

Imagine This

Can you imagine how differently mothers might parent their children when they feel supported, acknowledged, and loved? Mothers who are kind and compassionate with themselves are more likely to raise children who are kind and compassionate, both with themselves and with others. Can you imagine how mothers could help their children manage their stress and anxiety because they themselves are better equipped to manage their own stress and anxiety? Mothers who are happy and healthy are simply more likely to raise children who are happy and healthy.

Can you imagine how different mothers might approach their relationships with their partners when they feel connected, understood, and appreciated? Mothers who can communicate their needs and wants effectively are more likely to be in a relationship with less conflict, resentment, and feelings of isolation. When parents and children together can communicate better and understand one another more deeply, the compassion expands and their connection flourishes within the family.

Let's take a leap now. How about a world where *all* mothers have the self-care strategies to truly take care of their own emotional well-being? A world where *all* mothers have the communication skills to get more of what they want and need from their relationships? A world where *all* mothers have the emotional capacity to parent at their best?

When mothers are unflustered, *they* can flourish.
When mothers are unflustered, *their children* can flourish.
When mothers are unflustered, *their relationships* can flourish.

Imagine a tsunami for a moment (just the powerful mechanics of it, not the potential death and destruction). When an earthquake causes a tsunami, shifting plates in the Earth's crust quickly push up on the water above the quake's epicenter. With a speed of up to 500 miles per hour, waves expand outward in all directions. As these waves reach shallow waters, they begin to slow and compress. Seawater from the shoreline is powerfully drawn back into the sea, joining the waves and building to heights that frankly give me nightmares. But this tsunami doesn't represent a destructive force. No, it's constructive. In fact, it's very powerfully positive.

You, my friend, are the epicenter of a tsunami of *flourishing*. The changes you're implementing in your life right now represent deep shifts in your foundation. Your very crust is breaking and forming anew. When that happens, it doesn't just affect you. You are a different person now, with new insights, awareness, self-worth, and understanding. You have new skills and abilities that support you and allow you to flourish. When these changes raise your level to new heights, the impact quickly expands outward in all directions. Fast.

Your children and your partner will be the first to feel the tsunami of your flourishing waves. Families who understand and communicate compassionately with one another will experience connection instead of isolation, joy instead of hurt, creativity instead of destruction, empathy instead of judgment, and understanding instead of confusion. They will begin to truly flourish.

The wave continues to expand, gaining in momentum and power. Because when families are happy, collaborative, compassionate, and connected, their local communities will flourish. Their careers will benefit. Their financial opportunities will expand. Their physical health will improve, alleviating pressure on our health system and lessening the propensity to self-medicate. Alcohol, drugs, pills, eating disorders, and affairs all become less tempting when people have healthier and more effective self-care strategies at their disposal.

Then the wave expands even further. Entire regions will feel the impact when the communities within them flourish. The energy and resources spent managing discord, disconnection, and destructive tendencies can instead be used for creative efforts. When there is less to fix, we can build. When there is less confusion, we can see clearly. When there is less conflict, we can have more joy. When there is less anger, we can have more compassion. And what happens when entire regions are flourishing? Countries flourish. Continents flourish. The planet will flourish.

The incredible thing about this tsunami of thriving is that it continues to propagate itself not only over space, but over time as well. Children raised in families, communities, regions, and a planet with the capacity for self-worth, emotional well-being, and compassionate communication will, in turn, quite naturally raise a next generation with these qualities at their core.

This tsunami of thriving that will change our world and affect the generations to come begins with you. Today. I realize it might not feel like a tsunami at this moment. The shifts you're making in your life might instead feel like a tiny drop of water in a raging, uncontrollable sea. Even so, those drops begin to add up. And when many drops of water connect and move in the same direction, with the same intent, that force can be incredibly powerful. A constant movement of water can cut through mountains. It can carve massive canyons. It can topple structures that have existed and persisted for millennia. Your flourishing life can carve out a new path in the bedrock of humanity. Whether you're inspired to be a tsunami of thriving or you begin with one drop in the direction of the life you want doesn't matter. Either way, you have a deep power within you to affect not only your life, but also the entire planet for generations to come. It all begins with you. Right now. In this moment. Deciding to heal yourself. Deciding to be kind to yourself. Deciding to have faith in yourself. Deciding you are worth it. You deserve to flourish, and that, my friend, will transform the way you parent, partner, live, and love.

ABOUT THE AUTHOR

AMBER TRUEBLOOD, MBA, LMFT, is a licensed marriage and family therapist, bestselling author, speaker, and mother of four sons. She is passionate about helping moms get the tools they need to create health, wealth, connection, and happiness in their lives. Trueblood is the author of *Stretch Marks: A Self-Development Tool for Mothers Who Are Being Stretched in Every Direction* and has written and contributed to articles in *O: The Oprah Magazine, Bustle, People, Good Housekeeping, Parade,* and more. She has made television appearances as a featured expert on *E! Daily Pop,* KTLA, CBS, and *Good Day LA.* She lives in San Diego with her family and their cat Andi.